People don't drown in living rooms

People don't drown in living rooms

By

Orna Reuven and Yair Eldan

English Translation developed and edited by Michelle Mazor

IPBOOKS.net
International Psychoanalytic Books

International Psychoanalytic Books (IPBooks)
New York • http://www.IPBooks.net

People Don't Drown in Living Rooms

Published by IPBooks, Queens, NY
Online at: www.IPBooks.net

Photo Credits:
Orna Reuven by Dinozaura
Yair Eldan by Keren Ella

First paperback edition

ISBN 978-1-956864-45-8

To Hadasa,
From Yair

To my beloved parents, Zvia and Issac Reuven,
From Orna

Part 1
"Folie à deux"

1

Hello Ella.

I'm dying to see your face right now. How long has it been since we last spoke? Probably a year, more or less? How are you? Still working hard? Still teaching?

You should see me now, how I kept all the scraps from the floor of "the cave" and am still able to keep them together so that I have something to work with. And still after all that patchwork, the first thing that comes to mind when I think of you is persistent and unrelenting teasing.

There you go again making me think about sex. I know things about you, little tidbits I picked up along the way... that you have two girls, you're divorced and that you're an only child. But what's really engraved in my memory of you is how you used to sit there with your perfect fingernails, polished bright red, what else, as if from the beginning of time, and the smoothness of your shins... How I used to quiver at the sight of the moist intersection of your crossed thighs. I remember how I could almost reach out and touch that river of milk flowing next to me... and me pulling back. Always pulling back.

You're probably saying to yourself "there he goes again, his aggression is back", and you're right. I didn't even ask if you'd be comfortable with me writing to you. But you can relax—I'm far, far away in New York, and just like with everything else that happens to me when it comes to you, I feel as if you're the one who made me send this email. You have this power over me. The ability to pull my strings, even from a distance. I'll try to ignore that thought and take some responsibility, as you yourself told me to do many times. The days here in New York are wonderful. I try to jog in Prospect Park at least twice a week, and I tell myself, this is you, Itamar, and this is your body, and these are your obsessions, and these are your fears, yours and not anybody else's. So, this is me writing. The me who wanted to be seen with you outside "the cave", without your notes and interpretations. As man and woman. Not a day goes by that I don't think about how it could have been between us. How we would have had sex. How I would have fucked you until you begged me to stop. Look at what you're doing to me. For months I've been thinking what to write to you from this place, and in the end what comes out is the same thing that always happens with you, a volcanic eruption of tempestuous words. I can edit it. Delete everything and jot down a few lines like: "Hey Ella, how are you? How are the girls? And work? I'm fine, working hard but all in all, stable and satisfied. I feel that we left off on bad terms and I'd like to get some closure, can we talk?" Yes, had I written something along those lines, I would probably be a lot less threatening, but if I know you—and I do, I know exactly what turns you on. Honesty. Brutal honesty. So while we're being brutally honest, please don't lie to yourself thinking that you kept to the boundaries of the cave. I know you hate it when I call it the cave and we both know that you didn't keep to the boundaries. With almost every word that came out of your mouth lines were crossed. So what if you didn't tell me too much about yourself, or that we didn't really fuck, but do you really think that you can have that kind of control over me without crossing a line? All those funny words you and your colleagues love to use, trans-ference-shmansference, like it's a mechanical procedure that takes place in some research lab and not in a room with walls and a carpet and chairs and people with fingernails and hands and crossed thighs, where what really happens is an endless mating ritual — and mating is crossing boundaries with a capital C.

I see all those moronic intellectuals snicker: "Well well, transference. That's exactly transference!". So many lies they tell themselves, thinking they can control it, that they can quantify touch and words and information, failing to understand that when you put two people in the same room and they start talking, there are no boundaries, no boundaries at all, and it doesn't matter whether they talk, go down on each other or kiss. The wheels spin and spin and their matter amalgamate, simple physics. You can't even imagine how many boarders I crossed while gazing at you, how long it took me to work up the nerve to do it, to silently look at you, to imagine in meticulous detail how you chose the dress you wore, how you stood in front of the mirror and felt that that was the dress you wanted to wear that day; the top of the bra you chose peeking out from the cleavage, and your lips, entire days during which your lips would cross the border and reach me from the other side, from your beautiful, bountiful and polished country all the way to my wild, shapeless thicket.

So, Ella, you turned forty-one this year, right? I wonder how you look, if you did anything new with your hair, and what about your breasts... Just joking, what I really meant to ask is how you've been this past year, whether you're happy, and satisfied. Will you write back?

Itamar

2

Itamar,

I've read your email several times, feeling the surge of thoughts and emotions it raised in me each time. What a volcanic, accusatory, invasive, and painful outburst.

Indeed, our sessions ended quite abruptly a year ago, and it was certainly not the appropriate way to conclude such a meaningful therapy. It was your decision, and I respected it, but reading your email I am aware of how incomplete it all was.

Itamar, you remember that I repeatedly offered you to come back to our sessions if you changed your mind. You are still welcome to do this, we can find a way.

Do you even remember our sessions? The ones we were so versed in and could lean on for support and meaningful insight. But this—this thing you've unloaded into my inbox—this, no. I don't know where you came to the idea that it is allowed. Did our interaction somehow teach you this?

Ella

3

Pain. That's what I'm feeling. Not because you didn't ask how I am doing. It's your condescension that hurts. It hurts to feel you emotionally detached. It hurts to feel you alienating me. Are you seriously suggesting getting back to therapy? I'm in New York. Do you want to have online sessions? That's not even the point. I just wanted to talk. To write. Not therapy. I've asked you twice how you were doing, I asked about the girls, about work, and you didn't even bother to reply. What happened to you that made you change so much in one year? The Ella I remember had a response for everything. You used to stop me and say: "You asked me a question, right? So I would like to try to respond". And your forehead would slightly wrinkle as your hair flipped toward me, and I knew it wasn't only your soul attuned to me at that moment, but your entire being. You would straighten out in your armchair, cross your legs with those perfect high heels that I'd kiss if I could. Where is that Ella? And what kind of question is – "did I teach you this?" No, Ella, you did not teach me this. This is what people do, they look at each other and exhale and speak, and then touch. And it results in penetration, a rape, and the decision to define rape the way it is defined only shows that you've succeeded, you and your colleagues, in shaping the boundaries of the relationship.

But if it was up to me, I'd use completely different parameters to assess how dangerous someone is, how invasive. And actually, here in New York it might work, with all their fake smiles and personal space, but in Israel? Show me one person who has an issue with space. Quite the opposite. All I remember is bodies pressing against bodies, on the bus, in line at the post office, on the street. Remember that day during the bombing of Tel-Aviv, when the sirens went off in the middle of our session, and suddenly all the walls you built around you came crashing down? I found myself standing in a bomb shelter with you, your two girls and the babysitter. I was so happy, I thought I would explode. The youngest held your hand so tightly, she was crying, and you were trying to calm her down, and the older one looked and asked: "Mom, who is that?" And you answered, "This is Itamar, my friend," and you were beautiful, your maternal fingers wrapped around her hand with just the right amount of strength and slackness. The mark left on your finger by your absent wedding ring made my spirits soar, and at that moment I hitched my wagon onto a star, because friendship is the highest form of love, it has no benefit, only the desire to know someone and make them happy. That's the title you gave me – friend. When the sirens ceased, you had nothing to lean on, Ella darling. There was no protocol, no setting, nothing. The world had turned upside down. And I thanked each member of the squad that had launched the missiles that day and led me into that shelter with you and your girls.

I don't understand. What are you so scared of? What do you think would happen if you answer me like a human being, like a woman receiving an email from a man she knows is attracted to her?

The temperatures are rising here, and I have no idea how I'm going to survive the humid summer. The trees are giving one last bloom before withering, the fruits are heavy and ripe, the streets mercilessly bright and all of this is stirring a sense of discomfort inside me. Do you remember how I used to arrive at the office sweating like a pig, and you would look at me with disgust? I could see that you smelled the sharp sweat too. But what I know about you, that others don't, is that the more disgusted you are, all the more attracted you are. As if the sweat opens a door to something deeper and wilder, and you want to enter. So what's scaring you, Ella? Come in, it's only me, Itamar. I was never much of a match for you anyway.

Besides, something happened. There's a reason I need to talk to you.

Something happened, something from which there's no return, and the first person I thought to turn to, was you.

Itamar

4

Itamar,

I know it took me a few days to respond, and I'm sorry if this delay hurts you. If something happened and you need my help – write what it's about and I'll try to think it over with you.

I needed some time to process the medley of hopes and accusations you expressed towards me in your emails. I especially needed time to make sense of other sides of your anger. Because somewhere between the mating ritual, the rape, and the penetration into someone else's habitat, it's crucial to say that on the distant brink of your anger there is someone I remember well. And even though he's hiding under layers of desperation, envy, and contempt, I can see him there.

I must ask again, if you remember that man who used to come twice a week and share the secrets and inner workings of his heart? Remember how delicate the words were that we meticulously chose to convey our thoughts? Remember the shared ideas we created? like a language of our own. There is no need to twist and distort our efforts into classifications from a parallel universe. Friendship? Mere attraction between a man and a woman? Teasing? Coaxing to sex-talk? Reading these descriptions is making my heart cringe at the missed opportunity they convey. I genuinely hope that we will be able to have an honest conversation about what you truly have and lack in your life, and of what you truly had and lacked with me.

Ella

5

Hurt me? Yes, a little, but from where I stand the concept of pain takes on a different body and volume. The delay in your reply spurred a certain reaction, something moved at the tips of my nerves, and somehow now the common idea that there are no degrees of pain seems absurd to me. There are entire worlds of grief, buildings of pain and neighborhoods of agony, and it's not just their form but also the space they take up. Some are miniature, little dots, and others keep mounting until there's no room for anything else. Until the breadth of it takes up all space and leaves nothing for air. And you suffocate.

What hurts me is not your classic avoidance, that of which you have become so highly skilled, of talking and saying nothing, or of not being present while announcing that you are. Ella, we're also hair and legs and breasts, and idle chatter, and not only these empty cocoons, soul stripped away, until there's nothing left of the world within them. What hurts me is that you can so easily point out my aggression but don't acknowledge your own. You say I'm contemptuous, desperate, envious. Maybe. Contemptuous, for sure. I'm tired of being bound to the conventions of manners and etiquette. Desperate as well. I don't understand how life still exists in this ocean of desperation, so much life. Envious? I don't think so. That's yours. Why do you think I'm jealous? There, I asked a question in the language you want us to speak. I wonder if you'll answer.

Did you really think that you could start a conversation from where we left off? Those who live, who have real relationships with real people, know how important it is to start from these banal questions and not run straight for the soul's subconscious motive. Just look at my emails compared to yours. Size does matter. Remember what you said to me about my masculinity, when I told you how troubled I was about the size of my cock (and I apologize if I'm violating your holy principle of talking only about the here and now). I'll never forget how you flirted with me because that's when I knew there was a chance we could have a relationship outside of therapy too. First you took my hand and measured the length between its base and the tip of my thumb. You said, "That's how you approximate the size, and I'm telling you, yours isn't small". Then you said that every morning we see ourselves differently, and how elusive our perception of our body is, shifting every day and every hour, and that when it comes to size a lot of it has to do with my self-confidence. That day you wore your tight jeans and the thin white shirt with the hieroglyphic print, and every time you moved your hand I could peek a little further into the slit of the armhole, and I said to myself, Itamar, this woman is perfect.

You know what, Ella, everything you said back then was true, and it helped rays of light penetrate the dark dungeon I was trapped in. But what saved me, what really set me free, wasn't you. It was that woman who came on my cock, and at that moment I was Iron Man. Our conversations were like Tylenol, Ella, but that moment removed the tumor. You yourself once told me, with your bright red lips from the lipstick you had just applied before I came in, that sometimes one must act, enter the flow of life, not avoid it. You said that one should study towards a degree, get married, connect to some familiar human form in order to feel alive. My father had just criticized me that my life was going nowhere, that talent wasn't enough. "You're already thirty-five years old" he said, "you can't go on like this, asking your parents for more money". You tried to explain to me what he was saying. You said that life wasn't poetry but prose, that it's about people who act instead of just contemplate, and when you said that your mouth was in action, your cheek bones were in motion, your hand gestured to me so I could internalize what you were saying. And when you undermine yourself, turning your own words into actions, your voice into movement, it is as if you had made a pact with me. And only now do I realize that you were both siding with me against my father and taking his side, and that's exactly where I was, and to me at that moment you were at your most beautiful, your very most.

I'm tired. I guess you're not ready yet.

So this is it, here's the update of the past year. A year with a lot of pitfalls. I finally found a use for my American passport and arrived in New York in the winter. It was Freezing cold. I was supposed to crash at a friend's, someone I knew from back home. I called her when I landed but she didn't answer, can you believe it? Eventually I went to some youth hostel in the Bronx, and the following morning, Jess, that's her name, called me back. She had gotten the date wrong by a day and was out of town, and what a shame we missed each other. That was my beginning here. But all that doesn't matter now.

Thanks for your offer to help. Funny, your phrasing sounds so American, so perfunctory. In any case, I can't write what this is about, not here, maybe over the phone, maybe not even that, and please don't bring it up again until I mention it myself. I have reasons to be afraid.

I care about you, Ella, the place where we connected is rooted inside me, and I'm still feeding off it. I'm writing this in the event you decide not to write anymore.

I wish you only happiness,

Itamar

6

Itamar, I think it's time to set a few things straight. I'll try to make myself as clear as possible, and I hope the length of this email will be to your satisfaction.

I'll be very explicit in writing that I have never taken your hand in mine, nor have I offered my opinion about the size of any of your bodily organs, including your cock. That is such a distorted spin on what happened, it's as if we weren't even sitting in the same room. When you raised your concerns about the size and adequacy of said member, I told you I truly believe that men and women don't necessarily engage in technical measurements during an encounter. They meet. I said that I hope they attempt to experience the various levels and layers of their meeting in full, not in centimeters. You then responded with that far-fetched indicator you've now attributed to me, and I smiled at you and said it sounded a bit sad. How did you get from there to the heated, crude, disturbing recollection you described?

Utilizing this opportunity to its fullest, I would add that standing together in the bomb shelter was certainly a dramatic event for everyone concerned. I was under the impression we thoroughly addressed many aspects of it, including you meeting my two frightened daughters. You might recall I told my daughter that you will wait here with us, reassuring this shy and completely shaken little girl that I know you well. "Is he our friend?" she asked me quietly, and I nodded in encouragement, not grasping how strongly this particular gesture affected you.

Itamar, what will I ever do with you?

7

Dear Ella,

I thought it was possible, but I was mistaken, although I still don't exactly know where I got it wrong. One thing's for sure, we don't really understand each other, because if we did, something would have resonated. Which means, I guess, that I haven't seen you until now. I apologize.

I assumed that our sessions also created some kind of human connection that would enable us to talk like human beings. That's what I was trying to do, to initiate a normal conversation, not the kind we had either in your office or the "cave". It's hard to distinguish between the two. Maybe the difference lies in the tone, that thread that drives through the vocal cords, the neurons in the brain, and the feelings, and binds them all together. In our therapy talk, that thread was clear. In your office we explored how I felt, we examined what was happening and what it all means. The exploration itself was the primary objective, not you or me. In the kind of talk I wanted us to have, and I mean it, the goal was to connect our souls.

You remember the event differently. Maybe you didn't actually say anything about the size of my cock, and my memory of meeting the girls in the bomb shelter is inaccurate. But there was a crossing of boundaries there, and that's what I wanted you to address. Exploring the meaning of the "bomb shelter" in the context of therapy is interesting, even fascinating, certainly to you, but that wasn't my intention. I simply wanted to remind you

13

that the boundaries came undone, and if that be the case maybe there is a chance we can have a relationship outside our therapy as well. What happened is fairly simple – I asked, and you turned me down. That's perfectly fine. And I have you to thank for that, for knowing how to deal with rejection. Do you remember when I wasn't accepted to med school? you taught me that it doesn't mean that I'm worthless and shouldn't study at all. So a girl said, "You're kidding, right?" when I worked up the nerve to ask for her phone number. That doesn't mean there isn't some other woman out there who will be attracted to me. You see, you taught me well. I can handle your rejection.

Or maybe I'm wrong and it's not a rejection at all. Maybe all relationships start with a period of tearing down each other's resistance. Each one takes his or her sledgehammer and starts gently breaking the other's resistance. Oh but no, that's not the right metaphor. Too violent. I'm going over what you wrote again. Your words are psychologically tainted, not only the probing tone but also your tactics to break through your patients' resistance. You reveal a little and conceal twice as much, trying to seal the clinic off from the outside world, the patient sees you covering the windows with nylon sheeting, laying the blankets under the door, making it seem like a safe zone, and he lets his guard down, while yours is still up*.

Yes, you're psyco-babbling again. It's quite something, this osmosis. Like how someone who works with criminals becomes something of a criminal himself, or how someone who works with autism becomes a little autistic. Maybe that's how it is with psychologists too, maybe they start penciling in meetings with

---

* A reference to the Gulf War in 1991, when Israeli citizens were instructed to seal windows and doors in response to potential chemical weapon attacks by Iraq. A common reference to being naive and easily misled.

friends, and then end these meetings on an uplifting, diplomatic note, as they do in their sessions with patients. Language affects the way they perceive reality. But they fail to take into account that this osmosis works both ways, and then they fall in love with the patient. But not you, Ella. You don't fall in love. Love is for other people.

Ella, I'm lost. There's no hope for me anymore. I've done something from which there's no going back, something that penetrates every vein and makes me loathe myself, and I already know that if my reservoirs of self-love can run out so fast, there's no chance I'll survive. But you – you have your whole life ahead of you. If only the language you've adopted doesn't slowly kill you. Finally, the heart will demand its due, and all the psyco-babble substitutions will no longer satisfy it, and it will give up.

Once again, I apologize.

Hugs,

Itamar

8

Itamar,

Your emails worry me a great deal. I can feel how hard you are trying to reach me, but your way of going about it is so bitter, and so tangled. I think there is something you don't fully comprehend, or perhaps you aren't even aware of; in my eyes, the meeting between us was a blessing, it truly was! It brought with it a kind of human warmth completely absent from our writing, a natural curiosity, such playfulness with words...

This doesn't happen in every therapeutic relationship, just as it doesn't always happen outside in the real world. But sometimes, just sometimes, the door opens and a patient with intelligent pondering eyes walks in, and I know beyond a shadow of a doubt that this journey will be significant.

Obviously, the journey is a turbulent one, but that's okay, more than okay, that's the meaning of an authentic encounter with another. Meeting the psyche in all its forms of expression—in its superfluity, as in its deficiency.

Itamar, what has happened to you since you left, and what hidden request lies in this correspondence? I feel we're on the verge of toppling into something that's off limits, and you were right to say that I had set these limits when

9

My last email was sent mid-sentence, unedited, and incomplete. I tried to finish it Saturday morning, when the girls were riding some wacky alpaca in the desert, but it got deleted from my phone. So now I don't really know what you read and what you didn't, and this slip of mine raised two thoughts.

The first is directly related to my distractions; I reminisced about some of your favorite moments in our sessions, the moments you felt had somehow evaded a strict regime whose rules you didn't fully understand. Always ready to catch a shred of a smile, a surprised expression, a sentence that went off on a tangent, an inappropriate giggle, and most desirable – an untimely knock on the door, maybe the air-conditioning repairman arriving too early? And through whom you could discover something crucial that must be exposed. Nothing got away from you. Not the book lying open on my desk, perhaps it resides beside my bed at night? Or a half-finished cup of coffee, or the smell at the entrance of the office, or a chapter published somewhere, once even a different shade of eyeshadow – all signs, clues, designed to uncover the "true" Ella. Not the fake one, who is always composed and guarded from you. Moments that "reveal a little and conceal twice as much", as you put it.

What a shame, since this entire time I've been willing and ready to meet you; it's like looking for breadcrumbs scattered under the table instead of enjoying the bountiful meal we ourselves have set before us.

And why am I writing this? Because these past few days have been a giant mess, which you would have no doubt taken great pleasure in. What you wrote about holding hands and measuring genitals was unnerving. I could have let the whole business of staying in the bomb shelter slide, since everyone there was rather anxious (even you, Mr. Itamar, who thanked each member of the squad that had launched the missiles), but I won't accept the delusion about holding hands and measuring genitals. It shows a complete inability to differentiate between fantasy and the reality of the encounter. And since this inability troubled me, and I was upset and distracted, you got to read my unfinished email and maybe also a few sentences sent from a smartphone undoubtedly too smart for me. Do you really think this is the only way, between wacky alpacas and overly sophisticated smartphones, you can truly meet me? Only through my blunders, my digressions, my failures, and confusion?

This leads me to the second thing I had on my mind today, and it has to do with what might be the greatest confusion of all – this writing project we're both engaged in, as if it's perfectly reasonable and obvious for a former patient and his psychologist to correspond with such a sense of confidence and fervor, without taking pause to contemplate the nature of this thing that's happening here – a thing you so obviously want to pursue outside therapy, whereas I clearly want it contained to the boundaries of the space in which we met. So come on, Itamar, you're scattering breadcrumbs, tossing around names of women, worrying me that you're already beyond hope... put your cards on our shared table. What has happened to you since you stopped coming in for therapy?

Ella

10

You were with the girls at an alpaca farm? Where? Down in the Negev? Such a cute place. On a family outing, one Saturday, I took my nieces and nephews for a hike from the hostel to the farm, and when we got there an alpaca spit on little Noa. I told you about her. She was in total shock, but later we couldn't stop laughing about it.

You went alone with the girls? I can barely handle these smartphones myself. I've had so many embarrassing incidents sending texts to the wrong person, or the autocorrect completely changing the meaning of what I intended to say.

Reading your email, I laughed and cried at the same time. How incredibly conservative you are. How fearful. Maybe I've already crossed that thin line that distinguishes normal people from those who not only consider the social conventions to be ridiculous, but who are downright outlaws. And here you are, busy protecting your fine reputation. God forbid someone should find out a patient claimed you talked to him about his dick and accusations start flying, and before you know it, everything you've spent years building goes down the drain. So you solemnly clarify to your patient that it never happened, directing your words not to him but to the big brother who reads your emails. Funny. And sad. I remember I once wrote an email to someone who worked at a serious investment firm, something along the lines of "When will we sniff a couple of lines together again? I've got some great blow," and I accidently sent it to her work address, which is regularly scanned by the company's security department. I instantly got a phone call, and we drafted a reply together. She wrote: "Very funny, I've already told you, quit trying to talk me into it, it won't work..." And I wrote back: "Okay, okay, I give up, my tactics don't work on you..." And that way everyone calmed down. How funny. How sad. Just like your narcissism, which knows no bounds. You're the center of attention at all times. It isn't regular transference, to use you and your colleagues' terms, it's something more extreme with you, some kind of undocumented conditioning that happens to you the moment you enter the position. The unwritten rule that if somebody wants to be your patient, he has to agree that yours will be the dominant presence in the room. In that sense you remind me of Ruth, remember I told you about her? Ruth, who bound the love poems I wrote her and gave them to me as a birthday gift.

You're right, I tried to reach you through the breadcrumbs, because they are your only real characteristics. Hoping that something in your sophisticated system of being present and absent at the same time would suddenly malfunction, allowing me to see the true Ella. You delude yourself by thinking that you're conducting full, sincere encounters in the office – not just because it's impossible to maintain so many full and meaningful relationships at the same time, but for the simple reason that most of the time, you're not really there. Not as Ella. That's why these hints, which, for a fleeting moment exposed a part of you like some virus in the software, were so dear to me. And yes, when I saw David Vogel's *Married Life* on your desk, that exposure made me happy. There were times when we really met, I saw it in your eyes. Times when you understood me, and I you. It isn't for nothing that the cock grows hard in such moments, it's a testament to a real bridge being built.

The "writing project", as you put it, is our life. Have you gone completely mad? If there's one thing worth doing before the rope tightens around my neck, it's to wake you up. Ring your doorbell again and again. Maybe you'll awaken and find that the shadows you see are people, not blurry elements in some architectural sketch you need to polish and perfect. What are we doing here? I try and I try to lure you into a relationship with me, and you refuse. Maybe I deserve it. I was so full of resistance walking into your office. Weeks of beating around the bush until I was finally able to bring my body and mind to sit in front of you. And maybe that's why it's all happening like this now. Maybe that's the price all psychologists pay when they're out there, in the world: their patients' resistance translates into their own resistance to meeting people. All the energy they spent tearing down their patients' defense mechanisms, for which they had to enlist their own crazy defense mechanisms, leaves a void that seeks fulfillment in the outside world. Am I right, Ella? You know I am.

These past few days have been so hectic over here that I haven't even noticed you sent two emails and not one. The words got blurred in a screen of fog, which isn't entirely unpleasant right now, with reality being difficult. Very difficult.

It goes like this: I need a loan of about twenty thousand shekels (6000 dollars). I need it right now. Or more like yesterday. This isn't why I renewed our relationship, please believe me. This isn't a matter of taking advantage. It's something that came up these past few days and has to do with the situation I'm in. With all your resistance I'm sure you'll say no. But since I'm desperate, I'm asking anyway. It's a loan I promise to repay. If not me then someone on my behalf will repay it, maybe my parents eventually, but I can't ask them now. If you say yes, I'll send you my bank account details. And if you say no, that's fine too, we'll continue talking here.

Itamar

21

11

I find myself writing, rewriting, and moving paragraphs around, so I'll just answer the question you've asked me. I understand you've gotten yourself entangled in something that's very confusing and frightening for you. This must be the case, because your request for a loan is so entirely foreign to the landscape of our relationship. And since this request is so aberrant and odd, I'm asking you again to explain what happened, and why you can't ask the people who undoubtedly precede me on the list of potential lenders. I'm being honest with you, right now I just don't know what to say. If you're in dire straits then I want us to work together to see how I can help, I'm not sure that it will be what you had in mind, but we'll see.

This is me trying to respond out of a belief that this is a special occasion, leaving out most of what I feel about the endless testing of my personal and professional boundaries. Am I right in doing so? Am I foolishly following the breadcrumbs, instead of simply saying no? Because I certainly see your endless attempts to provoke and challenge me. And the measure of alleged sophistication you employ for these provocations; it's so transparent, but still manages to be incredibly exasperating. Do you ever wonder why you feel the need to annoy the people closest to you? As if ours is the first and only relationship on earth that is lacking, missing, asymmetrical by nature, and hasn't achieved a full realization of each and every aspect of it, including the physical one?

Argh, this is where I must stop. I keep on writing, and more openly at that, even though I know our communication has only one worthy and proper place. I don't even know if it is possible to be a "former patient", as I myself put it before. Anyway, I truly think this needs to stop.

Ella

12

Ella,

I'm so sorry for yelling at you on the phone, really... I was so frustrated and hurt. After reading your last email there were moments I thought you were a monster, and in order to overcome that unbearable feeling, 'to get it out of my system' as the Americans like to say, I called – but it was a mistake, our conversation went all wrong. I didn't mean to swear at you, but when I heard your soft voice and warm response, I just fell apart. What made me so angry and brought all those terrible words out of me is that duality of yours. It's so confusing to me. On the one hand you're so detached, and on the other so connected. How is that possible?

Maybe we're all like that. We take such a great deal of interest in other people while being indifferent to them at the same time. We're curious and interested and alienated at the same time, in the same world. Your messages are like that: sharp and precise but also vague and false. And yesterday those words of yours seared me, like a branding iron on pigs' flesh.

I didn't mean for it to come out the way it did, forgive me.

Anyway, before I forget, there's an important matter I want to talk to you about. I want to send you a small package. A bundle of pages by snail mail. Will you keep it somewhere safe? I'm trusting you on this.

Now I want to say something about us again. After everything I've gone through this past year, I truly believe that psychoanalysis was created by misanthropes with a special aversion to relationships. I thought you were different. But it's just the opposite. You, Ella, are the most dangerous type of therapist. I tried telling you that on the phone, but everything got mixed up, and I didn't say the most important thing. I'm not testing your "professional" boundaries. I truly do need the money and I truly will pay you back, and if I turned to you that means there's no one else who can lend it to me right now. Because I decided to live, to walk away from that non-life in Israel and venture into the unknown with two hundred dollars in my pocket and the flimsy promise of a relationship. I was sick and tired of all the endless reading, days on end, it was nothing more than jerking-off, and all it really conveyed is contempt and pity. I was tired of all those who viewed me as the guy who wandered off yet lingered at the yeshivas' lectern, contemplating the criticism of Rashi's commentary as if the answer could also serve to remedy his aching heart. That's it, I didn't want to read anymore, or to try to parse and zero in on the nuances, but to just live. To reach out in the middle of a session and caress your cheek, to act on my feelings as they come, without thinking about future repercussions and without fear of rejection.

There are moments in this life when you have to decide whether you're standing in place or taking the plunge. Whether you're soaring high or dragging your feet, whether you're living or dying. And when you decide, you decide. You can't keep sitting on the fence. My request isn't that strange. So a guy you've known for years is asking you for twenty thousand shekels, what's the big deal? Why are you so afraid of being exploited? It's so simple. If you have the money, lend it and I'll pay you back. And if you don't have it, then say you don't have it. And if you don't want to lend it to me, then be straightforward about it, and write the actual words "I don't want to lend you money because – ". Instead, you just perform your usual juggling act, zigzagging between all the possibilities without committing to any of them. You do your

"Argh, this is where I have to stop," with your endless flirting. Look at what you gave me: the dead end as well as the frustration, the sorrow and the desire not to stop. It's flirting, even you can't deny that. That's why it's only supposed "sorrow", supposed "desire". It's not real. I don't believe you.

I am sorry I annoy you. I'll give you that. Do you want to hit me? Slap me? Punch me? What do you want to do to me when I annoy you? Are you scared of losing the distance between fantasy and reality when you feel violent? Don't forget that I know better than anyone that every encounter with the world, imaginary or real, can be dangerous. Why are you stopping? And with me, no less, the one who feels so close to you?

Oh god, I just realized that you wrote that you feel close to me. How selective and pathetic is the human consciousness, how slowly the truly important information sinks in. I feel close to you too, Ella. And I am annoying. Yes, I annoy the people I'm close to. Maybe because I'm a walking defense mechanism and I'm so hard to reach, I can see all of your defenses. The patient assumes that if he can learn to lower his guard in therapy, to trust the therapist, he can do it in real life too. What a stupid, maddening assumption. After all, that's what the payment is for: to mitigate the risk. And the higher the payment, the more you believe you're insured against risk. And when that rarity happens and people do lower their barriers in real life, they immediately start to insure themselves with all kinds of secondary policies: "I can always get out of the relationship", "I'm still independent", "I've learned how to live on my own and trust myself," but if they could grasp what is really going on, and see that they are in a state of complete exposure, then the horror of their existence would crush them, because in this almost celestial state, a man is just a crumb inside the voracious mouth of the relationship. It is in this state that the seeds of change can be sown, that shapes can shift and interchange, but also a state in which you can simply cease to exist.

So what are you saying, that a physical consummation between us is impossible? Even if just in your imagination? And you found it so important to tell me this? You had to reestablish the power dynamics by displaying your sexual weapons? You know I fantasized about you because I confessed as much in therapy, and I also wrote to you about it. And I know you fantasized about me. A man knows when a woman fantasizes about him. At least that region of my male lobe is still functional. Why is that so difficult for you to admit, to talk about, or even just hold as a possibility? Why do you have to accumulate power when the whole point of a relationship is shutting down all the generators and relying on the more infantile, nucleus engine?

I had fun swearing at you. It made me slightly aroused. It wasn't planned, it just happened in the heat of things. I didn't mean to hurt you. I apologize. If you change your mind about the money, it's still relevant and would help me. If you don't, something will eventually come up and I'll manage.

Yours,

Itamar

13

Your ability to read between, above and below the lines, along with your belligerence and aggression, is truly rare. You offend and apologize in the same breath, and you know, Itamar, the only space in which I find any point or moral justification to listen to such words and think of them is the scope of therapy. There's no reason to let you experiment with such a sadistic attack in my email or phone. I will not let you.

So here is my last question: beneath all the swear words, I heard you say something in an almost off-hand mumble, you said you've been charged with sexual assault? Did you say the money is for a lawyer? Did I get that right?

Itamar, listen to me: I'll be in New York in three weeks for a conference of the Psychoanalytic Society (also "widely known" as the Ku Klux Klan, I get it). I'll be in New York for a little more than a week, and I can meet you at a friend's office. This will be my loan to you. We can meet twice or three or four times, and you can pay for these sessions later, or pay a symbolic fee, or not pay at all. It's a rather unusual arrangement, but I truly believe the best thing I can do is to give you time to explore what has happened to you, and to put our heads together to figure out how to deal with it.

That's it. That's what I can offer you.

Ella

P.S. In relationships we don't really rely only on the infantile, nucleus engine. We operate many generators, and there's no dishonor or insincerity in that. So come on, operate the infantile, nucleus, mature, evolved, peripheral, intelligent engines... we have a lot to figure out.

14

Must be fun living in your world, a world of closed spaces and transatlantic trips to conferences, a world in which you can extract evil and box it up, take it abroad (I bet that on the plane they label it "Danger – Hazardous Waste"), open the box, and examine it with the KKK's bomb squad. You've got a sense of humor, I'll give you that. You're crazy if you think I'll meet you at an office in New York. Even if it was feasible, and it's not, as you'll realize when you read the letter I'm going to send you by post. The only way I won't meet you is in a therapeutic setting. Why do you immediately run to that? And where did you get the idea that I was charged with sexual assault? I don't remember exactly what I said, but even when I replay the conversation in my head, I don't get that. Maybe you fantasize about me sexually assaulting you? Was that what you were dreaming about during all those long hours in therapy? With all the tension building up between us? I talked about it explicitly, but you? Maybe that's when you first had the thought that the only way to break through the formidable boundaries besieging us is through plain violence. That I would bend you over and penetrate you without asking a lot of questions. Without your consent. On the outside they would call it rape, but in your office, yes, in your sacred cave, it would simply be the way to blow up those walls, which had been growing taller as the tension between us rose.

And that fantasy also lets you maintain that vagueness you're so fond of. In your fantasy you resisted, after all, you said no. I'm the one who assaulted you. And that's real rape. That way you can be neither here nor there, the way you like. Not that this allegation is so far-fetched, because in reality, evil is distributed equally among everyone. It doesn't matter if that evil meets the standards of criminal charges and what they like to call "mens rea". At the end of the day every assault on one's freedom or body is equal. I can't write more about it now, but you'll find out for yourself soon enough.

You can be sure I'll meet you, you beautiful white racist, but it can't be in an office. I'll figure out how to schedule it. I'm thrilled that you're coming. Thrilled that I'm going to see you.

Maybe I wasn't entirely on the mark with the generator's metaphor. I didn't mean an alternative power source but rather the way people create noise and distractions in order to deal with the simple, clear-cut fact that they're dependent on someone else, and that their lives are in that person's hands.

Itamar

15

I can't go on.

You're doing everything within your power to drag me into a sado-masochistic cycle, and I have let myself be dragged in, because of my own tendency to insist on the wholeness of things, of you, of your therapy as well as of this.

I heard correctly what you said about a sexual assault and a lawyer.

I'm writing this with sorrow, with clarity, with acceptance – if you choose to meet me in an office in New York, or in Tel Aviv or even in Abu Dhabi, I think I'll always agree to meet you.

There will be no other kind of meeting, nor will I open the package you sent.

Ella

16

So that's what it was between us. Our relationship can only exist when you're in control. Only when you have the upper hand. Look at the premise you chose: only you get to determine the facts of my story. Maybe that's your motivation as a psychologist? To determine for others, in a winding, roundabout way, the facts of their own lives? I wasn't charged with sexual assault. It wasn't that. What's so hard to understand? And it's so fun to finally meet you, Ella. Hi, Ella. It's so real when you're angry and aggressive, undoubtedly the position that suits you the most. So, on your turf, I gave in and accepted your authority. No more. There's no sadomasochistic cycle here (more terms out of the KKK's play-book). The fact that you're so self-involved that you can't even see that we are in an actual relationship is profound. A distorted, unhealthy one, at least for now, but a relationship nonetheless. You make no effort to empathize, to support, and you don't have to. I wrote you that I can't come to an office. I'm not under arrest, but I can't come. I would be putting myself at risk. There, I wrote more than I wanted to. Happy now? You have power and influence over me. A lot. Even happier?

Go to hell, Ella. You and your therapy and your organic food and nice shoes and expensive skirts. You really don't see where I'm at? I'm going to send you those fucking pages even if it costs me my life. Don't open the envelope for all I care, and don't show me the kindness I'm asking via these pages and what's attached to them. It might weigh heavy on your conscience. That may sound dramatic or banal, but that's reality for you. There isn't, and nor will there be, a return address on the envelope, so if you don't accept the letter, it means I'm going to be in deep shit. Neck deep. And it also means that what's written in those pages, the hope that's still there, is a false hope, a lie.

Itamar

17

Argh, Itamar! Annoying, persistent, enraging, intriguing, broken, foolish, Itamar. What on earth do you want from me? What's that thing you need so desperately, you're willing to crush and pulverize and wipe out every strong and healthy part of me?

I can withstand a lot, but not everything. I truly believe you find this odd and surprising, so I'm writing again, point blank: I cannot withstand each and every thing, let alone all of them together. And you, like a clingy baby who bites the breast and won't let go, what do you need from me?

Our relationship was born in therapy, that's where it will live, and that's where it will die. That's the premise of our shared life.

18

I've just finished writing the letter, attached what I wanted to attach, and I suddenly realized that I forgot your address. How is that possible? After weeks and months and years of walking to your office, the same streets, same trees, same stone fence, same pavements, same entrance, intercom, stairs. I see them clearly and still I forgot. With everything they fed me, with their desire to erase what I used to be, what I am, I guess it worked.

I meant to send you an email and saw what you wrote me. Obviously, there is no god and no such thing as a mystical connection, but it is just as obvious that we influence each other in ways we can't even begin to imagine. Maybe it's not divine but it is beyond our grasp, surprising and pleasant. Only three minutes ago I wrote that I can finally see you in front of me, feel your empathy and the boundaries you set for yourself, for my sake as well as for yours. And what do you know? Only a few moments later, I'm sitting and reading your email – feeling us finally together. It doesn't matter how, therapy or no therapy, but together. Not through the words "our shared life" or "relationship", but through your questions, which brought tears to my eyes. Is that what I'm really like? I want to crush you, wipe you out? I hadn't even noticed that is what I do, all I wanted was to get your attention, to get your heart to beat in my direction. I didn't think it would be so unnerving, I thought it would build you up, make you stronger.

Finally, I also appear in a sexual context, even if it's just a baby biting the breast, but what joy it is to imagine myself sucking that pink, perfect nipple of yours, the one I could only imagine. I was finally invited a few more centimeters below that cleavage,

36

to follow the curves of your white bra, to press my mouth against your erect, beautiful nipple. I can't give you anything, Ella? I'm a needy baby who only takes and takes? When I suck your breast, I'll indeed suck it like a baby. And like a thief fondling a bag of diamonds just stolen in a brilliant heist, I will proceed with the same sense of ownership that comes with every babyish suckle. How did you even endure breastfeeding? I bet that was the only time you let yourself be robbed, allowed the world to leave you naked and bare.

I was tired at the end of the letter, and now I'm simply exhausted. The nourishment I've been feeding on lately leaves something to be desired. What I really need is for you to talk to me like you talk to yourself. For you to tell me the things you tell yourself. That's it. But if that makes you weaker, don't do it. You need your strength for your impressive juggling acts.

Suddenly those pages are making me nervous. I hope that when you read them, you'll go easy on me, Ella, be charitable like you are right now. You remember how the vapors of our sexual tension condensed between us in therapy, how intoxicating and stimulating they were? How you somehow managed not to reveal yourself and at the same time let me fall in love with you, leaving me exposed in my dependency, in my attraction?

I believe that the bond between us, the bond that is so vivid and potent in your email, cannot be undone and I choose to make it the foundation of our relationship. It may be an illusion, but I promise to build us up from here and from this moment we will sprout branches and leaves and from here will come the fruit.

Yours,

Itamar

P.S. Send me your address.

19

I want to describe to you what's been happening to me lately when I read your emails. I feel rage. I'm perfectly aware it's not the only or even the most comprehensible reaction one might feel. But I'm sitting with a fierce old rage that climbs up my throat like nausea. Sometimes it twists and turns and wraps around my heart. I feel the tension in every pulse as my blood rages and cascades into territories I didn't even know existed. It takes me a few moments to tame that feeling. I wait for this ludicrous feeling to pass.

The more we continue to write, the further away I drift from my base, from my simple truth. Hold your raging horses, it's hardly a confirmation of your view of the fundamental dishonesty of my profession. It's something else, more like an erosion, a gradual grinding that begins to cave in.

You see, the endless search for something you feel you were previously denied of: something is always missing, hidden from you, wrong, should have been different, and the intensity of the anger... If we were in therapy, I would let myself ponder: how this infinite insufficiency was created? Where do the roots of the betrayal go? Whose rage do I perform with such persistence? And whose refuted compassion do I offer once again? They are ours, yours and mine, don't get me wrong, they are the derivatives of our relationship, but do you truly believe they originate only there?

I see the parallel lines of past and present, yours and mine, they help me understand the injury and its ramifications. These are the contours of my thinking, for which you came to me. But in our writing, it becomes too blurry, so hopelessly mixed. In what sense does this constitute a "truer" me? All the efforts to subvert my role, to disassemble components of my professional selfhood, I feel they serve the opposite effect than revealing something authentic about us. I know that I become more vigilant, more stiff. I find it more and more difficult to freely think, to speculate, to work through with my emotions and ideas.

Just look at the words we exchanged; how an uncareful alpaca makes you swoop in on these meager tidbits as if hunting for a treasure (my fault), how a metaphor of breastfeeding becomes fucking (my fault?), nothing stays as thoughts to reflect on, ideas to breath in. Don't you miss therapy? the place where it is clear what's off limits and everything else can be playful and alive? Because what am I supposed to do, Itamar, when it's this bizarre extraterritorial correspondence, and phone calls, and mysterious packages, that enrage me? What could possibly be deduced from them? Besides a temptation to discuss what ought to be discussed, but simply somewhere else.

I can hear it, Itamar, in my words and in your cries for help which are becoming increasingly desperate, that you're drowning. Let me help you the way I know how, in my friend's office in New York. And please hold onto the package until we meet.

20

My very dearest Ella,

Ironically, it feels as if I'm the one holding the perspective, cradling it like a crystal ball. Living in awful conditions, having to hide until the storm blows over... it casts a new light on what really matters, creates a world in bold relief and everything is clearer, brighter, and sharper. I am the wandering Jew, the conscious pariah. Hannah Arendt was right, something about being an outcast makes you more sensitive. Despite everything, I have yet to withdraw from the world, I'm still here, still want to make a change, to make things better. You know me, I'm a nihilist, but now I feel less disengaged, less aloof. Maybe it's the eye of the storm, or maybe I'm just finally able to accept this world. Ella, I'm not bitter-sweet, as you used to describe me so often. You are. It's you. We haven't spoken or seen each other in a year, so I didn't know how to approach you, and I thought, intuitively, that some kind of an attack on therapy, as a concept and as a relationship, would do the trick. Why did I even have to bring up therapy? As if the possibilities of a future relationship between us are reduced to that and only that. Why couldn't I have just said straight up that I'm in love with you? That I want to hear your voice and know what's going on with you?

It didn't happen in therapy. There, you were indeed an object of conquest, another monument to pee on and mark my territory, and you taught me so well how meaningless and childish that is, and more importantly, how much energy it saps from me, energy that could have been steered to other places, places where I'm more present.

No, it came after therapy. The yearning to hear your smooth voice, your wisdom and seriousness that somehow doesn't take itself too seriously. We're actually quite similar, you know?

From how and where I am, which is a pretty bleak place, a little smelly, dark, hidden, I want you. My violence towards you, my retreat into the sexual, my blinded gaze, the axing away at your resistance, it all stems from the desire to break down the characters we had turned into during therapy. Therapy that was so successful it turned us into icons, frozen in space and time. I thought that in order to really see each other we'd have to shatter them, to free us from our cocoons. What do you say, Ella, do you think we can turn over a new leaf here? Why did we even paint ourselves into this corner? It's so simple, all I am is a patient who is reaching out a year after therapy has ended. Like a student who calls her professor a year after attending his course. Anything is possible. I narrowed the possibilities instead of widening them, and you went along with it. I guess I did it because I feared the possibility of a real relationship with you. I was afraid of what would happen if you lost your magic outside therapy, if we would lose the tension... the passion. And also, I have to admit, I did it because that's all I know. That's how we used to talk, and I used the same language, the same words. And we, Ella, we have to invent a new language here.

Think about it, we truly are free. I'm crying and laughing right now. I'm free, despite my ordeal and the fears, I'm free. Maybe not free like those who have money and can do whatever they please. I'm free like Auerbach, who wrote Odysseus' Scar while living in exile in Istanbul, cut off from everything he had known. He was surrounded by the books he loved, in the basement of a monastery. And that cliché, "free in spirit" – the one I used to

41

mock when I was younger, saying "who's free? Are the poor free? People who work from sunrise to sunset? People who spend their lives buying things are free?". As it turns out, that cliché couldn't be truer. Now I understand how much freedom a person can have despite financial and mental limitations. I was so free, even in the institution, even in solitary. But your freedom – that's a different issue. Who knows with how many chains you shackle yourself each morning. I know and don't know you. I know that it's important to you to have a successful partner. And now that you know my flaws inside and out, not to mention my current predicament and everything I've gone through this past year, how would you ever want me? And yet, I'm offering you myself and my love. It's okay if you tell me: Itamar, that won't work for me. It's okay.

Dear, sweet Ella, about the address. Is that another stunt, another way of stalling? Contact with the outside world isn't so simple these days. Every venture to an internet café, every run for supplies, is complicated, which is why I asked for your help. But I'll find a way to send you what I wrote. In the meantime, I'm offering you my love. I'm aware of the fantastical elements of this proposal, but at the end of the day, every proposal, no matter the context, has such elements. The thing is, and I've come to realize this in the past few months, our relationship is one of the reasons I'm still alive. And I want to cling on to you and to life.

A kiss and a hug,

Itamar

21

Itamar, something very bad is happening, and I need you to stop with all the masks and half-truths. I know you think you're presenting yourself to me at your most exposed, but that's hardly the case; I don't know anything. You're describing a dank, Holocaust-like hideout, and strange forays for supplies, and loneliness that sounds unbearable. How is it that you've become something of a refugee?

And I'm no less interested in what's going on in your inner world, which is muddled and turbulent in ways I fear I can no longer keep to myself. It's a rather deceptive crystal ball you're holding right now. I won't even go into the subject of your love proposals; this isn't the time for it. Somewhere inside your bittersweet mind you must still remember that a psychologist and a patient aren't akin to a student and a professor, and the type of roles we agreed to take upon ourselves aren't the kind that are transformed by time or circumstances (and regarding relationships between professors and former students, I sometimes wonder whether a decisive transformation in the dynamics is truly feasible and fair).

Itamar, I keep hearing you as if from the great depths, a secret message in a bottle that washed onto the shores of my life. Let's be honest and straightforward: can I contact the institution you mentioned? Can I send a psychiatrist, a friend of mine, to see you? It can be arranged today, and we can trust her.

I hope it's not a bait I'm taking, but considering the situation: 9 Rembrandt St., Tel Aviv.

22

Indeed, something very bad is happening. I'm going to have to change my email address and find a new internet café. I've been revealing too much in these past few emails and I'm pretty sure that either I've been found out or am about to be pretty soon. I'm sorry if that scares you. I'm scared too. I'm starting to make mistakes and am afraid of being sent back into the institution again, or maybe something even worse.

At the same time, I believe that something good is happening as well. Something very good. I feel you drawing closer to me, and I take that as your answer to my love proposal.

As much as I may be a refugee, I must say that despite the squalor and silent tears, I still feel that this place suits me. It isn't foreign, it feels right. Maybe I've read too many Holocaust novels, maybe it's in my blood. I am lonely, that much is true. I spend entire days alone. I don't hear my voice unless I talk to myself, still being careful not to make too much noise.

What I'm sure of is that I don't need therapy. A new relationship – yes. Certainly. Therapy – no. Maybe it's just resistance, but deep down I feel that I simply don't need it. I've already explained that is not why I reached out. So there's no need to send your friend to see me. I'm fine, thanks. About the institution, I wouldn't count on it. I sent the package to your address; when you read what I wrote you'll understand it's a bit more complicated than you think.

Ella, I wish I could say I'm sorry about barging into your life so crudely, but I can't. I wish I could say I regret making you scared, but I can't. It's true that I haven't told you everything, not only because I fear that my emails might be monitored, more so because of my exhaustion and inability to unravel the complexity of it all. There is absolutely no need to lift the veil or search for some missing half-truth because I was always myself with you, from the very beginning. I might have crossed the line for a moment when I asked you for money or when I was suddenly consumed by despair. But nothing more than that. You have nothing to be afraid of. This is my life and my mess as it flows naturally to my safe spot and puddles at your feet.

I wish I could believe that what is happening to me actually stirs something inside you. No, I'm not really that detached from reality. I know that for you it's patient after patient, and subsequently, empathy on top of empathy. How do you do it? If I were in your shoes I'd fall apart in an hour, because when I feel someone, really feel them, I can barely separate myself from them. I don't even think it's possible, what you do, taking them inside of you and what? At some point it can't stay inside, it must ooze out of you. Is that how you manage to go through session after session, day after day? I wish you were different with me. Don't forget to tell me when you're coming, and don't forget about the money thing either. Every shekel will help.

Yours,

Itamar

23

By post, hand-written

Ella,

I have no idea why I'm addressing this letter to you. You've already showed, time and again, your unwillingness to be involved in my life, and I keep dragging you in by force. This isn't really a letter, it's a report; and it feels quite comfortable putting your name as recipient because things flow naturally to it. I've used that name, E l l a, throughout this past year. You're the one I spoke to, the one I turned to, and I now know that this character I've been addressing doesn't really fit the real Ella. But that doesn't really matter to me. You're there in my mind, and my writing just flows. After all, I'm about to send you these words, this letter, this report, this chronicle—call it what you want—to your address, and you're about to read it. You, the real Ella. And now I can finally remember life itself and the strange, jagged chain of events I have found myself ensnared in. Everything becomes so clear when you're the addressee.

But reality is reality, and I want to ask you to put the letter aside for a moment and look inside the attached envelope. Be careful with the manuscript you find in there. If you have gloves around, I suggest you wear them, not that I was always that careful. Look at it, Ella, it's in German. I don't know if you speak or read the language, but this manuscript was written by no other than Sigmund Freud, and these pages came into my possession in a rather convoluted way, but they have come into my possession nonetheless, which means that through some inevitable cosmic event, they were meant to land in my hands.

Besides the monetary value (I've already looked into it, we're talking about a significant sum), it contains a secret that is about to shock many. And now that you know this, will you store the pages somewhere safe? In your desk? In your safe? It ought to be stored at room temperature, protected from heat and moisture. There I go stating the obvious, forgetting that I'm talking to the real Ella, who's more responsible and organized than me. She's the one I'm addressing, I mean you, and not the Ella who is the figment of my imagination.

I'm not asking for something criminal, it's entirely in the gray zone, and still, I'm asking you not to talk about it with your psycho-analyst or any of your male friends. I'll soon explain why. No one can find out about these precious pages. My life depends on it, quite literally.

Now I'm becoming completely irrational. On the one hand I'm writing to a fictional character, and on the other hand, I'm putting my life in your hands. You won't betray me, Ella, right? Neither the real Ella nor the fictional one? Even if you think I'm completely psychotic, you won't do it, right? No, I know that at the end of the day you'll have my back. I'm suddenly realizing how much my sexual obsession with you has prevented me from actually seeing you, deprived me of the ability to experience you as a human being; and now I'm simply imagining you walking from your kitchen to the bedroom with these pages, a person, a woman, sensitive and conscientious, trying to cope with everything life has dealt her. How insane that only now I can see you.

It's time to fall in line, to start over, if we can, me as a human being, you as a human being. All these stories about beautiful days in New York and jogging in the park are just that, stories. Lies. Sweet fantasies. I'm hiding out in an abandoned basement in Brooklyn.

There's a neighborhood co-op supermarket nearby, they bring in the supplies through the stairwell right by the basement, so I'm pretty set for food. The walls give off a sharp smell of dampness, but the days are getting hotter so it's really not that bad. It's rectangular, the basement, a shape that somehow relaxes me, there's order to it, but not a square, stifling order. When I got here everything smelled like piss and I even found a small pile of feces at the far end of the room, but that was already two weeks ago. Wait, two weeks? Maybe more. I've done a little cleaning up since. Every now and then I hear voices of people outside, and I curl up in my corner, praying I won't be caught. I've discovered that people like to stand by the basement door and talk, as if they're on the threshold, about to descend into the under-world. There, on the doorstep, they feel comfortable exposing their true selves. After they leave, I stretch out on the floor, and can breathe easily in my home again.

This is where I've been since I got out of the institution. The first email I wrote you was sent from the internet café on the corner. But I try to go out as little as possible. Officially, and I guess unofficially too (I'm just trying to calm you down, but what's the use, I've already crossed every line there is), I ran away from Bellevue. In Hebrew, the name Bellevue looks like gibberish, foreign and severe, but the truth is, in English it's soft, rolls off the tongue, and is considered a reputable place. Maybe that's why Jess thought involuntary commitment was a good idea. I didn't blame her at first. I was in such a bad way that I viewed any show of attention as kindness. I had forgotten how society could crush a person, shatter him to pieces. A day after I landed in New York, Jess and I went out for coffee. This was almost a year ago. At least ten months. When I try to replay the events, especially what happened that night, I always think about Meir Ariel. His songs got me through

48

my military service, made the daily grind less grueling. A Song of Pain relaxed me. As a student in a yeshiva, I hadn't ever heard the song, and it put the political conflict of the country into context, both a private and national one, and it got me through that period of my life. I'm writing this because I think that on that night I was left utterly bare. Without any perspective, without any sides at all. Suddenly I was suspended inside reality without the ability to see. Stifled. It's funny, but the judge in the hearing reminded me of Hagi, my company commander in boot camp, a determined, self-righteous, scrawny thing. I didn't stand a chance with him. Or with her. Jess was so persuasive, such a heartrending sight. If I hadn't known the truth, I would have fallen for it myself.

This is where I owe you an apology, Ella. I was institutionalized because I assaulted Jess. I don't believe there's a difference between plain assault and sexual assault, it's all about power and control and the obliteration of what is human. Poor Jess. Screw Jess. I unleashed my wrath upon her. That sentence, it's so very accurate. I mumbled it for a month, maybe even in my sleep. I looked at my hands, turning them over, and I couldn't believe what I had done with them. It's incredible how a person can empty his reserves of anger onto someone. Jess is an aggressive, indifferent, and insensitive person. But she didn't deserve me pushing her against the wall and strangling her. She didn't deserve me grabbing her crotch, didn't deserve me hitting her. No, that's mine. I flipped out, and Jess just happened to be there. Her behavior was the straw that broke the camel's back: I couldn't contain any more indifference, distrust, or exploitation. She didn't deserve it, but it was also inevitable from the moment we met. And forgive me all the bleeding hearts out there, but the moment I choked her, pressing her against the wall, something in her eyes lit up, as if she'd been waiting for years to elicit this reaction from the world and it finally happened. Freud wouldn't have raised an eyebrow at this, nor, in all likelihood, would he have thought me psychotic. Only a society that likes to sweep aggression under the carpet, as Freud himself argued in Civilization and its Discontents, would treat me that way. And there's a reason I'm bringing up that book, because the pages in the envelope I sent you are the original manuscript, which I'm currently using as a statement of defense, and hoping you won't judge me harshly. It's a statement of defense because all the layers of cultural pretenses simply dissolve when you feel that someone's taken you for a ride, been treating you like you're her pet. So you show her what a real animal is.

Ella, I haven't told you the whole truth about Jess. I first met her in Israel a week after I quit therapy. She's one of those girls who doesn't give a fuck and gets whatever she wants. She was about to move, and I was her pre-departure screw. It was all perfectly clear, completely open, and I felt honored that she had chosen me. She has that ability of making you feel like it's a privilege to be with her. I'm putty in the hands of those kinds of women. What's great about the institution is that there are barely any women like that there, beautiful, proud, the kind who take what they want whenever and from whoever they want. When I wasn't kept in isolation, I would stroll the garden and see a few of them there. Like a monkey in a cage looking at giraffes strutting the field. It was so beautiful there; even with all the suffering I couldn't help but notice it. A fresh and manicured garden, and in the middle of Manhattan no less. You probably think I'm just pretending not to notice the difference between plain assault and sexual assault, but I truly think it's one and the same, a body is a body is a body, and I hurt her, and when I put my hands around her throat it was just like trapping her pussy, pardon my bluntness, under my palm. The same control. The same desire to shut her up.

To conquer her. To make her a little less condescending, a little more humble, a little more respectful of the human race.

I felt that I was teaching her some humility. But her revenge was so sweet. She took such pleasure in the entire process. Had she opted for the police and prison route instead, she wouldn't have gotten half the pleasure she did from all those phone calls and hearings, determining whether I'm psychotic or not, dangerous or not, and she knew I was alone in the world, alienated from my parents and sister, and was at her mercy. At the hearing my fingerprints around her neck served as a frame for the face she put on, so concerned and terrified, you could almost hear the pieces of the puzzle snapping into place in the judge's mind when he looked at us. She sat there with a silk scarf around her neck, like a movie star, and had probably practiced removing the scarf with a casual stroke, revealing the marks my fingernails had left. The judge couldn't see, not even for a moment, that he had become a supporting actor in her play. She also knew about my American citizenship and social security, so it was perfect for her to stick me in a university institution where all my expenses were covered, and she could monitor the torture and methods of oppression from up close.

She never lost control. You see, between the two of us, Jess is the psychopath. Someone to whom social conventions do not apply, someone for whom human emotions, fears, hopes, are amusing at best. You're probably thinking that I'm suffering from major paranoia, but I'm telling you, one meeting with her and you'll see what I'm talking about. When you and I met for the first time, way back when, in your office I felt that you'd be able to dig deep and get to the source of the pain, and that it would benefit you as well, make you more human, somehow. With her it's something else. You'd see right off the bat that it's a different kind of structure; inexplicit, inaccessible – not because it's too stiff or has too many protective layers, but because Jess exists outside the sphere of interpretation, she's a type of disconnected being in a self-sustaining loop. And here I go, interpreting. How human of me, how wrong.

That's how she got me, piquing my curiosity, manipulating all that's human in me. She knows how to mimic any human response, but there's always some gap left between her and the emotion. Maybe that's what attracted me to her – since there's nothing to interpret, there's no effort involved. But it boomeranged, and now the effort has to be made, recalling what she said, remembering a hand shifting, a side-glance, the way she flicked her hair. The beauty of it all dawned on me during those long hours confined to my room in the institution, when people are faced with such horrible danger, they know it, they just know it. Our every instinct alerts us that we're facing a predator. I knew. And yet, I did it. I lowered my barriers, exposed myself. Like visiting the site of a radioactive leak.

At some point I'll write you about everything that happened in the institution, because despite the freshly cut grass and innocuous women, there's no point denying it, it's a prison. Now you see why I can't meet you in Manhattan? I'm a kind of fugitive. Being deemed dangerous is what landed me in the institution in the first place, and now, if I'm not there, it's prison for me. A real prison, with locked cells and guards. For people with normal lives, I'm the scapegoat. My weakness, my financial destitution, my solitude, all of it pisses them off. That's why no one had to think twice. I was my own worst character witness. Even worse than Jess. Two hearings were enough for them to put me behind bars with Feinberg, a Jewish psychiatrist, who I'm sure would have collaborated with the Nazis had he been born at the right time. He would probably have been the head of the Judenrat, sending more and more Jews to their deaths while stuffing his face and drinking, beating people up, and walking around like a god. He and Jess got along like two peas in a pod. I know that when he met her, she pretended to be worried about me. Maybe they even slept together. Maybe in his office, where I had to sit during our insipid sessions. It sounds like them, but I admit I don't really know. I'd prosecute them both under the Nazis and Nazi Collaborators Punishment Law, those two psychopaths.

I'm tired, Ella. I'll write you some more about my experiences, but for now I'm simply savoring my freedom. Enjoying it. Look at the manuscript. That idiot Feinberg kept the book in his library. He wasn't really interested in books, he inherited them all from his father, who seemed to have been a loving, empathetic figure, or at least that's how he's remembered on my ward; I asked the nurses. His photo hangs in the hallway there, staring back at me with benevolent eyes. Feinberg Junior is a whole other story. He'd make me wait in his office for long stretches of time, with a ceiling camera swiveling 360 degrees. He'd watch the patients waiting for him, pacing the room, embarrassed, annoyed, swearing. He took pleasure in it. Not one of them noticed his camera, but you see, in this case my paranoia saved me, and I spotted it in action. In some odd twist of fate, which I'll tell you about when I have more energy, I snatched those pages you're holding right now. At first, I thought I was lucky to get my hands on such a manuscript and get back at that ignorant asshole Feinberg, but later I came to realize that what I had was much more than that.

I initially thought it was just a first edition. But then, when I compared it to another copy, I noticed the discrepancies. Not that I knew the essay by heart. But of course, a pretentious idiot like Feinberg has all of Freud's writings in his office. So I was able to compare. In the version that became famous, after Freud asserts that the commandment "Love thy neighbor as thyself" is a response to human aggression, and that civilization and religion's attempt to ease this aggression only causes people to hate civilization and all it represents; and after he claims that the cultural principle of "Love thy neighbor as thyself" is illogical because "homo homini lupus" (literally – man to man is wolf); and after he writes that changes ought to evolve gradually and enable a fulfillment of instincts without civilization falling to pieces, without trading instinctual fulfillment for commandments that only show us how untamed we are, and how much effort it takes to restrain us – after all this he claims, in the penultimate paragraph, that he can offer us no consolation, just as the wildest revolutionaries and the most virtuous believers cannot. And now read further and notice another sentence, written in a different ink: "However, neither brings satisfaction to man like the understanding of his own aggression, the reasons why other human beings reject him, and the way in which the soporific drugs of religion and the revolutionaries work." Do you realize what's going on here? I highlighted the word "understanding" for a reason. I have no idea why it wasn't included in the published edition, but right after he claims that he can't rise before his fellow man as a prophet, in the very following sentence he in effect argues that psychoanalysis can replace religion, not only conceptually, but in its influence on the mind.

You probably think I'm overreacting, but... at least I noticed it. It's strange, but when I found that sentence in the manuscript, I felt as if it had been delivered to me by the hand of God. I read it as if it were written for me, as if my story could have ended differently. And that's what inspired my escape. Feinberg probably noticed the interest I took in this book. Because what he really loved that psychopath, was looking at the monitor, seeing his patients waiting for him, pacing the room, approaching the library and perusing his books. And that's just one more reason to take precautions. After reading that paragraph by Freud, I felt that I was once again part of a big, human mass. I forgot the wretchedness of my impossible situation. I knew there must be a reason I had found this sentence that was edited out of every edition. That I was meant to discover it. Not that I'm in favor of therapy the way you see it, with its scientific pretenses and boundaries. No. I simply remembered that's how I felt after our sessions, that I was once again of human form, and could actually feel my organs realigning and doing their job. If you've made it this far, know that there hasn't been a day when I didn't think about you since we ended therapy. Funny. Pathetic. I started this letter with some fictional character and I'm finishing it with you, I can actually see you before me, your bright eyes, pinched nose, calm and throaty voice, your deep empathy as well as those boundaries I hated, which you had set for yourself, for my benefit, and for yours.

Yours,

Itamar

24

Itamar,

Too many days have passed since your last email. I haven't forgotten about you, nor have I stopped worrying. Someone died and it's been a very difficult and exhausting week.

I'm still coming to New York, and I will read the pages you sent me by post before leaving.

I'm writing and deleting so many things. Hang in there,

Ella

25

Someone died.

Someone was here and is no longer. You're left with a memory. A voice. Images. A short sentence that comes through like a blurry image from Mars, implies how important this someone was to you, as well as how – well, there are two options here: how far I am from you, or how much you compartmentalize the chambers of your heart. I am indeed far away. Will we really see each other? I'm reading it again, you wrote me "hang in there, please." I'm reading your concern.

Ella, I wasn't sure you'd agree to stay in touch after you received the package. But you wrote me, and you're worried, and you even mumbled something about an address and a meeting, and that tells me there's a chance for us yet. That you aren't pulling back. I'm guessing you were brief because you don't want to reveal too much. And there's that someone who went and died on you. I always wondered how you manage it all. Work work work. That full appointment book of yours, which you used to leaf through when we scheduled our meetings. Not here. Not here. Maybe here. Finding an empty slot for me. I remember that powerful session during which we talked about my mom. Afterwards I leaned against the concrete wall outside your office, mulling things over, looking at the bougainvillea in full bloom and suddenly I said to myself: she spends all her time working so she won't need her mother. At all.

I look like a slob. I have to do something about it before you come. I don't want you to see me like this. You know how I'd stress out before our sessions, trying to make myself presentable, to narrow the gap between your elegance and my slovenliness, some kind of indication that we have a future.

I'm sorry to hear that your someone has died. That someone dear to you is gone.

A kiss and a hug,

Itamar

26

I'm so happy you've received the package I sent. Will you keep it safe for me? That manuscript could really set me up after this nightmare is over.

27

Itamar,

There are so many words to be written, I don't even know where to start. I'm in Madrid, waiting for my connection. Actually, "waiting for my connection" is a good way to describe the situation. The airport here is huge and almost entirely empty. Once, many years ago, I sat here with my mother and father. I'm so tired that I don't mind sharing this with you. My mother took out a bag of squished sandwiches she had brought from home, and I blurted out in an adolescent huff: "Good thing you have those, you don't want to be stuck without food in the ghetto," and pointed with my determined little chin at the dozens of colorful, fragrant food stalls all around us, tempters of Jamón and runny cheeses. And she, my poor mother, confused by my impudent use of the word ghetto, thinking (hoping?) I was asking whether we had a baguette, started rummaging through the bag in her frantic, flustered way, trying to save us from some horrible fate, not realizing that she was subjecting us to it with her frenzy. And then, then something really strange happened: suddenly she understood her mistake and instead of crying she burst into laughter. Laughed and laughed until tears appeared in the corners of her eyes, because she could never go completely without them. So no, Itamar, I don't work so hard as to not need my mother. She comes to me in many of my sessions and some sessions revive my need for her, which is boundless and sometimes erratic.

I'm reading what I wrote, and I sigh to myself: so this is how you write to me, without restraints, free of social, professional, and ethical conventions. You simply write freely, spraying your words on me, your love, your desperation. When I write to you I'm constantly on guard, holding back, biting my lip, counting to ten, to a million, reminding myself of my role. But what is my role now? Are you my patient? Will you let me treat you? Forever and ever and always?

I'm tired of death and panic. My mom went and died on me, and when the Shiva ended I ran away from home and flew to the conference in New York, which is a terribly irrational thing to do, and leaving my daughters like that... but what could possibly make sense (and I know this is an infantile thought) when the womb that bore me is inside the ground, and the disgusting chicken and rice she herself made is still in the fridge?

Maybe we are all just losing our minds from loneliness, crying out for a mother who won't come, forever and ever and always.

Ella

28

Ella,

Your mother died. I murdered my mother. It's not quite the same. Although, at the edge of my psychosis, in the last centimeter of my sanity, there is still a modicum of integrity within me that acknowledges that after all, my mother, that body I came out of and fed from, is still alive and breathing. Do you remember I told you she always used to talk about her leaky breasts when she came home from work, while I always thought about baby Itamar, waiting and waiting for a breast that wouldn't come?

I don't know why I can't just start by offering my condolences. Say that it's a difficult situation. That from here on, nothing will seem the same. Why do these words sound false to me? In such moments I wish I could feel like normal people do, those who can talk about their sorrow and excitement without feeling phony. And you even feel guilty for fleeing to your conference. I have no idea how you survived the shiva. All that silencing. Idle chit chat, heaven forbid you should say how you really feel. Fuck the world. I remember when my dad was told that his mother had passed away. The moment that rendered him an orphan. If I had found the strength to focus on that moment, maybe my relationship with him could have been salvaged.

Look at the glass half full. Now there's finally no one to let down. You're already writing more freely.

To be honest there's not much hope here either. The half-empty glass is always out there, the people who molded us, those with whom we had made blood pacts, whether lurking as shadows or ghosts. It's not for nothing that I've been talking to you these past months. Talking and talking with you. I think about you, sitting there all by yourself at the airport. A lost girl drinking coffee made to her meticulous specifications, eating a baguette sliced thinly as you requested with a hand gesture and your broken Spanish. Because that's how I imagine you, even though I've never had the pleasure of drinking coffee with you, and maybe you're actually fluent in Spanish, who knows? But I think that this, all the new information you dropped onto my lap, is going to poison our relationship. We're suddenly being carried aloft on a giant wave, and this wave is your mother's last breath, her halting heartbeat that's tossing us around like a rollercoaster. And this power that freed you to write what you feel, that jumbled your past with your present and let you speak your true self, this power generator is your mother's death.

You're probably sitting cross-legged at a small round table. Men looking at you, a beautiful, solemn, intelligent, lustful woman trying to shrug off death. While I, as usual, am being self-absorbed. I remember your sweet voice, "Not everything is about you, Mr. Itamar." Don't you deserve a few moments of grace? You're the one who told me that a relationship is measured by these moments of grace when judgment is suspended, when we hit pause, hug, and try to understand. But maybe you can't do yourself that kindness.

I really don't understand how you hung in there an entire week like that, with all those people coming and going, the mirrors covered (did you cover the mirrors, Ella? Did you follow protocol? I bet you did), all that talk and the photos and the smell of sweat. I bet the only moments you managed to think clearly were in bed before you fell asleep. How can you fall asleep like that, without a mom, without a defined outlet for the anger? What do you do with it all? It probably pours hot into your bed, drenches the sheets. But that's what's good about my basement, it isn't out in the world. I haven't thought about my mother since the moment I went down those stairs. The funny thing is that in the institution, which is supposedly cut off from the world, I thought about her all the time. Maybe that's why I feel I don't need rescuing. Not in the way you think I do. Actually, this is me inviting you to join me in this underworld I live in, a world in which the drops of salvation come from below, not from words or thoughts.

Everything I just wrote seems horrible to me, the insensitive language of a numb being.

I'm excited about our impending meeting and feel guilty about this excitement.

Ella,

The truth is I don't know what to say.

I'm sorry.

Itamar

29

Sometimes you're just unbearable, or a lot sicker than either of us are willing to admit. Probably both are true.

30

I know my earlier response was a gut reaction which obviously snared you, as such an enthusiastic advocate of authenticity, but did you really have to forgo all filters when I raised a bruised and battered voice? Really, Itamar? The fantasized murder of your mother, the description of things leaking and pouring, I can't endure it right now, I won't stay in the wild terrain of your words.

Sometimes I feel like an unwitting Little Red Riding Hood, hopping in the woods with a basket full of good intentions. I said I'd help you. I promised to help. And I'm a good person, and not a completely shitty psychologist, I can't just walk out on you.

But you can't have everything either. It's perfectly okay if that makes you angry, but we're going to have to return to the boundaries within which I can act.

My friend's clinic is at 200 Central Park South. It's on the corner of 59th and 7th Avenue. Yes, it is truly a fabulous location, and if you feel like commenting about rich people's smooth soft hands and goddamn institutions, you're welcome to it. I'll be there tomorrow morning from ten to twelve, and the doorman will know you're expected. My friend, the psychiatrist, will be there too. No one will expose you, and you'll be protected by medical confidentiality, but you should know that.

31

No.

No.

That's the word you hate most. And use the most. Your mother's word. It's not obvious straight away. On the contrary. To the innocent bystander it seems as if you say "yes" to anything. But a mother's word sends its roots deep. Anyone who knows you, knows how firmly that "no" is rooted within you. When you use its twin sister, "yes," almost immediately the tables turn and that "yes," which comes from the depths of your soul, becomes a "no," and what is left inside your mouth is yes and no. Yesno.

I wish I could take it upon myself and say "it's my fault", that I'm the reason you take one step forward and two steps back. I am guilty of my aggression, but this thing is yours. Yours and your mother's. You're the wolf, not Little Red Riding Hood. You're the one who doesn't believe it's possible. Not in any setting, whether it's near Central Park or in the center of Tel Aviv.

You are also Little Red Riding Hood. It's true. That's how I saw you. I once told you about my childhood in Beersheba, the sweet humidity hanging in the air, the sound of girls' flip flops against the asphalt, that feeling of remoteness, a wasteland of constant summer. Days were great as lakes, and clear*, as David Vogel

---

* From "The Dark Gate: Selected Poems by David Vogel", translated by A.C. Jacobs, p.9, Menard Press, 1976.

wrote in his poem, many dreams were dreamt there in secret, but no one listened, and life was for living but nothing more. There was neither past nor future, everything was in the present, such innocence. You weren't captivated by Vogel's poems of childhood but by his novel "Married Life," which so often lay open on your desk. You were probably drawn to the guile, the cheating, and the violence, and yet to me you revealed a different side of yourself. Not exactly Little Red Riding Hood, but something close. I recognized, for fleeting moments, a depth in your eyes that exists only in children. A depth of time unbound, of sorrow and joy in one, of someone who has herself experienced similar days.

Most of the time you're "no", but in therapy you become a "yes" with every fiber of your being, because only there you can be. But in real life, too, you can choose to free yourself. Yes, Ella, go on, free yourself. You're grieving, your mother has just died, and someone comes and unloads his trash on you, and you don't want this, so walk away. No one will blame you, you're doing everything by the book, I'm sure. But instead of walking away you ramble on about your humanity and your professional integrity. Who do you think you're fooling?

You don't have to set boundaries for the simple reason that the boundaries are already there. Primarily, we have skin that covers our flesh, orifices that open and close. However I may penetrate you, it won't be the monstrosity you envision, threatening to ruin you from the inside, a Trojan horse. You're you and I'm me. I don't confuse the two, you see? Once again fear and fantasy brush up against each other, and I'm sorry to disappoint you but your latent fantasy that someone will manipulate you and suddenly you'll find him inside you, is not about to be realized. The dynamics of power and control have become the compass of our relationship. All the needles point north only when you're on top.

But the inescapable fact is that in a relationship, you sometimes find yourself at the bottom.

I feel physical pain knowing that you're here, in New York, that we're breathing the same air. I didn't think it would get to me like this.

Ella, I'm repeating the obvious. I can't schedule any kind of appointment here with you, certainly not one that includes a specific time and location.

I know you still want to meet. I'll find a way. Not on my terms. Not on your terms. On both of our terms. You in your grief. Me in my hiding.

Itamar

32

Itamar,

Between my mourning and your hiding, my visit to New York is rapidly coming to an end. There have been quite a few moments when I thought I spotted you, turning a street corner, approaching the café where I sat and read, surprisingly joining my afternoon stroll in the park. I admit to locking eyes with a homeless man more than once, returning his inquisitive stare. You prompted the feeling that this is what I should be expecting. Maybe it was the way you described your lair, almost like something out of Amir Gutfreund's "Our Holocaust," and your effort to clean yourself up in my honor. You sent out signals. But to the office – to the organized, worthy, proper, feasible meeting – you didn't arrive. Just like that old children's song – "I waited and waited, cried and cried, for who has not come? Michael"*. It was one of my favorite songs when I was little, I felt deeply connected to it, even though there was no special Michael I was crying for (I'm reading this again and thinking: just a general state of endless waiting for a kind soul. Wonderful).

There's something improbable about the thought of leaving New York without having the chance to tell you the things I believe must be said in person. Had we met, I would have told you that everything happening now has a visible side and a concealed side, one that's hidden and private, even idiosyncratic in nature.

---

* Based on "Michael", by Miriam Yalan-Shtekelis.

Our relationship has a visible side, in which you're my patient who's reaching out to me in a time of need. But in the concealed side of the relationship, thunderous, bewildering sounds rumble, a muddle of mothers, children, and big bad wolves.

Let's take a moment to think about what happened with Jess and with the psychiatrist you mentioned in the package you sent me, whose name I won't repeat here so as not to expose or worry you. On the perceivable level is your assault on Jess, of which I will need a lot more information. For now, I'll just write that I know your anger, but I also know how you've handled your vulnerabilities until now. After this event you were sent to a psychiatric hospital for observation, I'm not completely sure what had happened in court before that. I understand that during this period of observation you came in contact with a psychiatrist, in whose office you discovered something interesting that you took away. You escaped from that hospital and have since been hiding in some basement in Brooklyn. With all its vagueness, this is my understanding of what happened on the perceivable level. But on the hidden level, something even more tormenting and tangled has happened, something you fear no one can help you with, since no one has your best interest at heart, everyone is either an ill-wisher or simply selfish, leaving you completely on your own. I need to ask you again to let me help. To that end, I'm asking you to look at the long relationship we've maintained throughout these past few years and make an effort to trust me when I say I'm on your side.

Although I won't be staying in New York for much longer, I know people here who can help you. We might view them as an extension of me; they could be your connection to the outside world, and I'll think about how to help you reach out to them. Also, the psychiatrist who treated you in the institution is someone I can talk to. I don't know him personally and haven't contacted

71

him, but I can schedule a meeting and try to understand what can be done. After all, you don't intend to stay underground forever, right, Itamar?

Over these past couple of days, I've been sitting at FIKA a lot; I've got a strange feeling that somehow you know this. It's a little place with amazing Swedish pastries, and tomorrow afternoon I'll have a few brief goodbye meetings there. 41 W. 58th St.

Ella

33

Maybe I'm tired. Craving human interaction. The mere mention of a café with pastries and goodbye meetings is like a bolt of surging sweetness straight from my old life. Meetings like these carry such force, like the trips we took after high school, huddled in sleeping bags in the desert, or by rivers, human energizers that left me brimming with life. And now, from the depths of my solitary existence, I intend to come have that coffee with you. And I hope that by virtue of my love for you we'll have a chance to talk a bit before I'm taken away.

The visible and the hidden level. I'm willing to play along. On the visible level you're helping a former patient in the midst of a paranoid breakdown. Despite his violence and vulgarity, you're still hanging in there, making an effort, offering your help. On the hidden level, for you this is a matter of life and death. You're a survivor. It's not for nothing that you've made it this far in life. And now all your therapeutic techniques serve to annihilate whoever stands in your way, whoever threatens to destroy you. You don't pull any punches. Who could identify this level? What will I say when they catch me? That you've betrayed my trust time and again? That you don't have a real conversation but rather pluck whatever detail suits you? That everything you write to me is made out of the stuff of your life, and that you're treating it like a crapshoot? That's how I feel when I read your emails, that you're having fun. And it doesn't matter what I say, my words will just become further evidence of my psychosis.

The number of people I trust in the world is zero, which isn't the same as saying I don't trust anyone. Because there's always some flickering hope that maybe, just maybe.... But there's no one. Even now, after your betrayal, I'm still here, waiting for that one person, that one woman, to at least have coffee with, the hopeless romantic that I am.

Ella, Michael didn't come, he won't come. It's the waiting that defines you. I'm guessing it's something that happened to you even before you were a little girl, something that happened when you took that leap of faith towards your Michael – and fell on your face. And since then, you're on standby. As we know, every event that occurs in our formative years plants the seed of a mighty tree. That should be enough for me. And it will be enough for me if, despite everything, all your barriers and defenses, you understand me. I don't need the world to understand me. As far as it's concerned, I'll always be the psychotic, misogynist, vulgar assailant. But you? You understand. I think you do. After all, you're still here. In my most troubled moments, I think you're here because I'm a juicy case that could bump you up the professional ladder. But most of the time I believe you're here because I'm telling you things you understand. You object. Refute. But you get what I'm saying.

So I'll be there. We'll have coffee and Swedish pastries and talk about grief. My grieving. About hiding. Your hiding. I used to think that after a betrayal one kept up the relationship in order to exact revenge, to restore the cosmic balance. Now I understand that closeness is not an expression of love but the thing itself. And I love you, Ella. For the first time, I'm not trying to justify or excuse this thing. All my rage towards Jess came from my love for you, like a current passing through a battery in the wrong direction. Because this closeness can assume all kinds of shapes and forms, and after letting out that rage on not-so-miserable Jess, it took me some time to realize what it was. That's also when I stopped wondering why I love you, a question I kept asking myself in each of our sessions, trying to convince myself of the fallacy of this love through all kinds of transference theories. Your mother's passing opened a small window. And this window, a porthole into our ark, showed me what we could have had, even if that window came at the heaviest price of all. But maybe that's what proved to me how real our connection is.

Itamar

34

If I didn't meet you, I would write that these stale power struggles are getting boring, as if people have nothing better to do but check who's on top and who's on bottom. I would write: if you don't want my help, fine, don't take it, but why does it seem so important not to accept it, as much as it seems important to offer?

And then we met.

When I was a little girl, I loved Erich Kästner's books, especially "Anna Louise and Anton" and "Lisa and Lottie." I used to relish the sweet, outdated translation, full of 'frocks' and 'stuffed pancakes, how horrid!'. I know it might seem an odd timing for stories, but bear with me, it helps me grasp all that has happened. And since I know you didn't chance upon such characters as the separated identical twins Lisa and Lottie in the holy scriptures of your childhood, I'll tell you more of how I coveted these girls' lives when I was little. Lottie lived with her mother in Munich, Lisa with her father in Vienna, and one summer they met at the girls' camp on Lake Bohren and discovered their parents' secret: "It was as though they were each discovering a new and strange continent. They had found out that what they had known up to now was only half a world."* In a wild, adventurous, and probably ill-considered move, the twins decide to trade places and travel at the end of the summer to the other's house: while Lisa acts as a little housekeeper to her busy mother, Lottie devours stuffed

---

* Lisa and Lottie, Erich Kästner, translation by Das doppelte Lottchen, Publisher New York, N.Y.: Avon Books, 1982, p. 29.

pancakes at the Hotel Imperial. In one of her conversations with their father, he tells Lottie, whom he believes to be Lisa, that he has decided to marry Miss Gerlach. When he leaves the living room he hears a desperate cry, as if his daughter is drowning. But once he reaches the hall and puts on his hat, he says to himself: "People don't drown in living rooms."* Often this sentence pops into my mind, and I think to myself: of course people drown in living rooms, and in kitchens too, and certainly in children's bedrooms, without anyone noticing.

That's how you struck me when we met again; drowning on the street in front of the Swedish café you wouldn't dare enter, submerged in a bile of panic and desperation, tired of longing for a pair of kind eyes. I didn't even think before taking you to Sarah and Jeff's nearby building, where they let you wash and shave in the bathroom and get you into the clean change of clothing Jeff loaned you, old man's clothes ironed to perfection. My kind clever Sarah, my reserved soft-hearted Jeff, together they had you looking like yourself again, while sending me on silly errands, so I could breathe.

As I returned with some food and the right size of shoes, you were standing with them by the beautiful bookcase. Once, many years ago, they fed me as well, and washed my clothes, and introduced me to a whole new world lurking in their library. A little waif found in a strange new continent. In every person's life there comes a time when someone just has to come to the rescue, I know this well. Is this why you wrote to me, Itamar? Is this why you insisted, like a fussy child, to detail and determine the exact kind of help you would receive from me?

I'm gathering my scattered thoughts, knowing there are things to be done now without delay. This is not the end of it, Sarah has

---

* Lisa and Lottie, p.88.

some ideas for us, and you are not alone in it anymore, but I must make sure you remember I'm going to Boston tomorrow to give a lecture I couldn't postpone, and from there I have a flight back to Tel Aviv.

Farewell, Itamar,

Ella

35

I bore you.
We met.
I drowned.
Savior.
I'm a baby.
You have a lot of words but no time.

And I'm the one initiating the power game? Maybe it's the grief, which you won't talk about, that drained you of every last drop of curiosity. Or maybe it's just all those years in your practice that left you hollow. You write. You treat. You toss the dice and toss them again. You tell yourself life is a game. And there are rules, without which you would remain empty handed. Without which there would be no meaning to what's happening here.

I'm still blown away by the way you looked. The short dress. Skimpy. And those heels. No one would have believed you're from the Middle East. You're an Italian who vacations in New York once a month. I let my gaze linger on you, letting each and every look enter my bloodstream so I could carry you inside me. And I'm still looking. Your new hairdo. The way it reveals your neck. I'm not sure I like it. I'm also not sure I like the simple gold earrings adorning your earlobes. Don't get me wrong. You fit right into the café landscape. A perfect fit. I bet it would look just as natural in Milan. But I know where you're from, Ella. You're beautiful in that look, and distant, and the years have left their mark on you. You're not a young woman. I can see it clearly now.

The danger accelerated and slowed everything down at the same time. Knowing there was only limited time was somehow both galvanizing and relaxing. Yes, I very much wanted you to take care of me. Sarah and Jeff, they were indeed there. The timid bourgeoisie. Manhattan caricatures. My "co-caregivers." The moment they stumble across some beggar they feel the urgent need to wash their hands, rid themselves of any connection to him. Bentham was right. Encountering a beggar on the street reduces the happiness of the passersby. Beggars equal pain. Prostitutes equal pain. The disfigured equal pain. Bentham had never heard of the far-better plan of the bourgeoisie: instead of confining beggars to the workhouse and have them pay for their room and board with the sweat of their brow, you simply give them, if only for a fleeting moment, the feeling that they are human, before sending them on their way. And the beggars, they're so stunned, such is their yearning for touch, for care, that they don't revolt; they receive this momentary attention and stumble off in a daze. That kind of morphine shot would lull anyone. And it really was fun to feel, for a few moments, like a human being. I have Jeff to thank for that. What wonderful small talk. The weather, the Democrats' views on Israel, racism in America, in Israel. I felt like a regular Joe Blow, to use my dad's expression. And you stood on the sidelines, and you saw that I was capable of communicating, capable of being your date at a cocktail party, of belonging. You saw it. For a split second. You felt it.

And then the "goodbye". Farewell, Itamar, in polite American. I won't dwell on your chameleon-like qualities, how you fit in so easily wherever you are. It's your survival skills and your therapeutic capabilities. What I'm talking about is how you say goodbye. That's where you falter, tongue ineloquent. Maybe it's your guilt that keeps you from saying things as they are, as they're meant to be said.

I met with Feinberg this morning at his office in the institution after the brief court hearing. Did you contact him? Not that I expect straight answers, but maybe that's the only thing I have left to expect from you. Everything looks pretty much unchanged here in the institution. Maybe a few new faces, but the place remains the same.

Who knows if that small kernel of trust, from which life can grow, still exists inside me. I'm not sure. Feinberg is going to make sure that kernel withers. In that sense, you're in very bad company. Even Hobbes, the worst among the lot, believed authority is subject to consent. Here I am again, and all that bullshit of the *cogito*, and man as a subject and the categorical imperative, it makes no difference. Philosophy halts at the institution's gates. I'm not sure that idiot even knows what I took from him and what he still has.

Ella, I've had enough. From here I move on. Far away from you. Our relationship meant the world to me. You will always be dear to me. Despite your treachery. I loved you just the way you are. Take care of yourself. May God comfort you among the other mourners of Zion and Jerusalem.

Itamar

36

Oh please.

37

That's it, Ella? Really? That's it?

38

I sometimes wonder how other psychologists would react to you; would they put an end to your tactics at once? Would they find another way to interpret your infinite longing for, and repetitive biting of, the nourishing breast? Over and over again, yearning and ambivalent, in a manner that keeps this love-hate relationship so troubling... Would they be able to explain it in a manner that would reach you and truly change something, shape new connections in your brain, pump new blood into your heart, awake you?

I know you're scared to death of being readmitted, but I don't believe more of the same talk is doing any good. And however difficult it is to let yourself contemplate the things that came up in our conversation, and actually feel the feelings that Sarah and Jeff's parental care provoked in you, I hope you will.

I think all the time of how we eventually met, how readily you let me lead you to the entrance of the grand building, where I nodded encouragingly to the doorman, hoping he wouldn't delay us, wouldn't stand in our way of a safe haven. How you let Sarah and Jeff peel off the signs of your escape, the hiding out, the hunger, the exhaustion. Itamar, how did you go like that to an internet café to write to me? And what places sent you away, only for you to misdirect your anger and send it my way? And all that time, while Sarah and Jeff gave you a "makeover," while keeping me busy with errands so I could come back somewhat reconciled, all that time I thought about my grandparents taking into their tiny Tel Aviv apartment their relatives from "over there", human brands plucked from Europe's fire. Washing them and feeding them with measured portions, absorbing their night terrors into their own bodies and souls, and their little kid, my mother, was there too.

When we finally sat in Jeff's study, I couldn't tell if you were more familiar than foreign, so I listened quietly until within the warmth of this wood-paneled room, I felt the chill of your Brooklyn basement. Itamar, you can trust Sarah and Jeff, I know this from my own experience, and when I'm back in Israel they will continue to help. While I was sent on needless errands, did they tell you anything about themselves? about us? Both are very dear to me. They were inseparable childhood friends, "forever and ever and always" is actually their saying, and they kept their friendship throughout life's upheavals, through careers and marriages, through bereavement and widowhood. Jeff was a professor of literature, Sarah was a psychiatrist at a university hospital, both are wonderful teachers, to me as well. They are long retired, and in the beautiful study where we sat, Jeff writes, and Sarah occasionally gives consultations. It was through Sarah's connections that we were able to get information on what happened to you.

I'm adding a few words now that I know for sure I can stay a little longer and take my return flight from New York. I'll be at the hospital tomorrow morning to see you. Sarah thinks I shouldn't stay, and God only knows why this feels a little as if you won.

39

No, you won.

In so many ways.

Back in therapy, and now too. The continuation of our relationship, after all, is predicated on my defeat. You therapists give it all kinds of sweet euphemisms, defining false consciousness and resistance and transference as if these were different types of winds blowing into your ear and settling in your soul, but the simple truth is that you demand defeat. One side must be vanquished, beaten, crushed to dust. I'm not surprised that this is the preferred modus operandi of therapists, because what is your office, Ella, if not a sparring ground in which there is room for only one Lady and one Peddler?* Until he is overpowered, this peddler; until he is tired of begging, falls to his knees and surrenders himself to her in obedience.

You think I'm in the institution again, just another one of your obedient patients. But that's not me. Maybe for you, and only you, I could have kept up this charade. I could show up at the institution tomorrow and make up another story, just to be admitted as an ordinary patient, sedated and fogged up. But I've grown weary. The phone calls Sarah made yielded the information I was after. It's more proof of the efforts I've invested, those that have already become a part of me. And then you, of all people, suddenly surprised me. You crossed a line. These are exactly the

---

* S.Y. Agnon, "The Lady and the Peddler", in *A Book that was Lost: Thirty-Five Stories,* The Toby Press, 2008.

kinds of moments I'd relish in therapy. All of a sudden, in a show of madness, you change your plans, arrive, and do exactly the opposite of what's expected of you. Now you're with me, truly with me. Suddenly there are no sides, no winners or losers, only the two of us against the world. I'm tired. You truly did win. In some roundabout way, you won. You can pat yourself on the back. Maybe not so much a knockout but in points. You defeated me, you beautiful, crazy lady.

Indeed, I looked like a homeless person. And if you think that someone can look homeless without actually being so, you're wrong. This mistake is the only justification for your behavior. I really was all those things. I really did sleep in a basement. I really did wear rags. I really did eat leftovers from the crates behind the Co-op. The only little or big difference, that gulf standing between me and a real homeless person, is that measure of hope, the possibility of slipping out of this costume at any given moment.

It turns out that it isn't that easy. So while you thought you were dressing a homeless, bathing a lost soul, in my mind's eye I was still the same. But you set signposts leading the way back to civilization, you really did do all those things, all *that* was real.

And I really did attack Jess. I left marks on her. I beat her. She told her friends on the swimming team that she had fallen. Or at least that's what she told me. Just like a battered wife. And yes, I know that's not so far off. And yes, she also pressed charges and now I'm awaiting trial. But she didn't have me committed. That's just my story. The more basic, simple truth also has to be said – I didn't stir up this drama for fun. Drama is the only thing that would have brought you to me because you need it, you feed off it; without it you're too much in control, too cerebral and calculated for me to steer you in my direction.

I'm the treacherous one. It's true. I'm not where you thought I was, and I'm not swallowing the meds prescribed by your friends.

But don't think for a moment that this detracts from your own treacherousness. From your seduction. None of my ploys can chip away at what you are. I'd venture to say that treachery and seduction are every therapist's lot. Maybe it's your secret handshake. Those who know how to cheat and lie with therapeutic affectation may enter your gates, the slogan proudly displayed at every conference – "Welcome, treacherous and seductive therapists!" And you take such pride in it because it highlights how "self-aware" and "sensitive" you are.

I have no idea how you'll react to what I did to you. I realize this isn't some party prank, a playful ruse in which you're informed of a delegation from England arriving to review your expertise, and you appear at the appointed time, prepared, having brushed up on the English terminology, open the door and I'm the one standing there, flower in hand, and you say: but there's a delegation coming, and I say: I'm the delegation. This isn't the case. I understand the difference. I'm not sorry. I came to understand long ago that the distinction between reality and fantasy is arbitrary. What we have is real.

Where will you go from here? Now you know everything. I'm still in New York.

Yours,

Itamar

40

Itamari,

Distinguishing reality from fantasy isn't always that easy. I get what you're doing and understand your need for it, but I also want to tell you: enough, let it go, it's me writing to you, not Feinberg. You're asking where I'll go from here? I'll keep visiting you at the hospital until my familial obligations force me to return to Israel. Maybe by then that healthy kernel inside you will grow, and we'll be able to think together of the next step. In the meantime, Sarah has asked the head of your ward to allow us to continue our correspondence, for the sake of treatment continuity, I suppose, or something similar.

We'll talk soon,

Ella

41

I deserve it.

And no one punishes like you. Who taught you? Your mother? Father? Yours are sophisticated punishments; the thought of being your spouse is downright terrifying.

Look what happened with the pages I sent you, maybe the most important pages ever to land at your doorstep. You haven't said a word about them, as if they too were mere fantasy. And suddenly I'm thinking – I did send them to you, didn't I? I placed them in a stamped envelope and sent it, I'm almost sure of it. Yes, one of the most important rules you therapists have is to never validate the patient's feelings. At first it really does provide the soul with some solace because the patient has to listen to himself. But this self-listening also melts one's resistance. Because our sense of normalcy stems from those same words our loved ones whisper in our ear, that assuaging incantation that means you're human, and what you're feeling was felt by other human beings before you. But the patient keeps talking to himself without getting any feedback, the threads of his thought entangling, and then he believes he's even more disturbed than he thought and that maybe he needs even more time to listen to himself, and all you do in response is nod, say yes, and how does that make you feel, and by doing so you push him even further away from the feeling of normalcy, of being human. All he wanted was to be told that his voice doesn't sound like a snore or a bray, that it is clear, coherent, and even if it's a loud cry, it is still of the human variety.

And once again you throw the ball back in my court. Should I wait for you in the ward? Stand at the entrance and try to convince you that this was all an elaborate scam I concocted? Would you believe me?

It turns out I have to go and complicate everything. To aspire to be with the most complicated woman in the most complicated relationship. And for what? I could have found that same erotic tension with someone who hates gays or thinks every Arab wants to kill us. With that kind of woman, I'm also guaranteed good sex. The difference of opinion would be balanced by the physical connection, and the desire to change a mind would turn into aggression between the sheets. Well, at least until penetration. You remember how much we used to talk about my anxiety surrounding the act of penetration? Hours on end in your office. And what's happened since? I'm fully functioning, that much is true, but the anxiety hasn't abated. It's there, growling like a caged beast, a bear waking up from its hibernation to find that its cave has been boarded up. I choose emotional tension instead, which can also generate good, wild sex, but never entirely drains from the body, it always leads a life of its own, tearing you up inside.

What does it take to be in a relationship with you? What would it take to convince you of someone's love? What would he have to sacrifice? Reading this, you probably notice that I'm completely sane. Stable, maybe not entirely, but stable enough. Here I go digging myself a grave again. Ella. Ella. Ella. How long until your kids can't do without you, until you start losing your balance and go back to them? Tell me, so I can prepare myself for yet another goodbye. I'll be at the entrance tomorrow. You can judge for yourself.

Itamar

42

I don't want to write about the things you do and say when I visit you. Inside the ward, outside the ward, inside your head, inside mine. I want to write about something else, about the frontiers of our relationship, about the outlying areas – the very areas in which someone must cease to exist for the other to thrive. Of course, we can address the belief that in order to truly meet me, you must lose your mind. In my honor and for my sake. But let me describe things from another angle, from your constant demand that I will cease to exist as your psychologist, almost as if the psychologist must die and a woman be born. With us, nothing seems to stay multifaceted, with its lasting complexities and swaying shades. This notion of a life for a life brings out of us nothing but the hardest materials, close to the tips of our nerves. It isn't coincidental. It speaks to our most basic human experience.

When teaching my students, I call it "terms of endearment" – the unique terms characterizing the foundations of the psyche. At times, violations of these terms happen; what was very much needed wasn't doled out regularly, not enough or too much, or just at the wrong time. We learn to live with these breaches, the psyche hardens and ossifies around them, like a petrified tree trunk uprooted by the wind, like a shell around the intruding grain of sand, like a broken bone.

You see, we all learn to live with the absence, with the excess, with the injury, but there are moments when something is too painful, too evocative, and the scar splits open, our faces contort with defeat, the old rage resurfaces. In our case, I think our terms of endearment somehow perfectly complement each other. The materials we wish to feed off, to spew, to spit out, to ingest, to hand over – they complement and feed each other. And the more you want to be, to live, the more I must be demolished. And it probably also works the other way around.

When I arrived in New York, motherless and enveloped in mourning, Sarah held her arms open and said to me: Now's the time to be patient and mindful, because everything's exposed underneath that brittle skin of yours. For therapists, she said in her responsible tone, this might be a challenging time, prone to judgment errors. Because patients feel the injury, some will dive in, each will attempt to make his own sense of it.

During that same conversation she gave me a book by a psychiatrist friend of hers, Glen Gabbard. When she retired for her nap I went to the park, sat on my favorite bench next to the zoo and read it, and I knew it was Sarah's caveat. No one knows my terms of endearment as deeply and thoroughly as Sarah.

Gabbard's book was about therapists who have abandoned the ground rules: giving their patients free sessions and money, inviting them into their homes for dinners and social gatherings, becoming their friends, sleeping with them. Gabbard wrote that these therapists were, for the most part, keen professionals (yes, you can smirk if you want, but I'm trying to understand the difficult cases, in which people cannot be considered systematic abusers of human ethics). Gabbard suggests that these therapists have stumbled upon a mutual trap, a two-sided destructive invitation. For instance, a desperate suicidal patient meets a psychologist who has just experienced a devastating loss. One is already willing to give up, the other is longing for reparation, I guess both of them are. In these situations, pain cannot stay as it is. Painful. Something has to be done. Maybe the psychologist feels he has to prove that he's not the abandoning parent who long ago betrayed the patient in the childhood drama. He's different, he will spare no effort, he'll do anything it takes. Anything? He then corresponds with the patient's almost hopeless demand for a proof of a life worth living, with someone who will go to the ends of the earth to save her. And it becomes impossible to breathe, right? As the analytical space collides into their realities.

I apologize if this sounds like a lecture in psychoanalytic psychotherapy. For me, these words resonate in a truly deep and healing manner. If you want to know me, as you say, that's where it lies. I'm a motherless daughter, a motherless mother, and all my vulnerabilities resurface with you. Many times I feel as if I have to defeat the turmoil between us, the concessions and cessation between you and your mother, the envy and hatred between me and my mother. And in the background, like an almost muted note, I hear my voice telling me: In thy blood, Live. I don't even know what that expression means, or why we say it on Passover. I know it has something to do with the earth being commanded, perhaps even sentenced, to welter in its own blood, in its pain. You probably know what it means, but I have no intention of delving into biblical exegesis. And yet, even without knowing where this expression comes from, it suits me, suits us. Because you're asking me to live in your blood, but I shall live in mine. You must understand there are things in your inner world, as well as your outer world, that I cannot change. And I'm sorry, Itamar, but I want to heal, I want to shed the veil of mourning, and soon I'll want to leave this place. Our time is running out. Will you wake up from your hibernation, Itamar?

43

I'm not sure I know how.
I'm not sure I can.

44

Wake up, Itamar, you can hear my voice, can't you?

45

Your voice is trying to persuade me that I'm asleep, but I'm awake in every sense. Maybe one can be both awake and asleep, a sort of reversal of The Song of Songs – the heart is asleep and the body awake, the way I felt with Jess. But not exactly. When we kissed I would close my eyes. And then open them. And that's where we met, Jess and I, our bodies at their most wakeful, until she averted her gaze and I thought she was consumed by pleasure. It wasn't a union of souls, that much is true. But our eyes said it all: you need me to be like this now, and I'm willing to be that thing for you. And vice versa. That's manifold for you. Not a connection of souls, but also not something limited to the body.

Ella. My dear, kind Ella. You have no idea how much I appreciate all the attention you're showering on me. It feels nice, it's flattering, it gives me the energy to wake up in the morning.

I'm not asking you to stop existing as a psychologist or a lecturer. But I certainly wish you'd stop existing as *my* psychologist. And that shift, which initially seemed difficult, now seems impossible. You're the one who dragged Gabbard into this, using him to tell me: this is what I'm doing now, treating you, without boundaries, going above and beyond, carrying out the mitzvah of charity until I max out my account. And that's what I've been saying all along that therapy is a relationship like any other, with only makeshift boundaries. And like in any relationship, those who lose themselves inside it are doomed.

What are my terms of endearment for you? It's hard to say. I was so busy drawing your attention towards me, getting you to trade your status as "my therapist" for a new one, and all that energy I've generated created a fog around us, leaving me without a sense of your needs. But from within that fog, my terms of endearment for you rise like two domed towers breaking through the clouds.

The first tower houses your wisdom, and my admiration for you.

The second tower houses your beauty, and my attraction to you.

Be whatever you want to be with me. Be my psychologist. Be a strong woman. Be gentle. Be an orphan. Be a daughter whose mother was made from her rib. Turn the tables, again and again. Be the same daughter of Israel whose parents, Amorite father and Hittite mother, cast her into the field, where the Lord finds her and tells her, In thy blood, Live. In thy blood, Live*. Be like her. Don't be like her. Whatever you want. You can assume her form, as she was perceived by the man who found her several years later – ungrateful, treacherous, promiscuous. You can resist, show him how his damaged masculinity, his unbridled jealousy and posses-siveness stymie the relationship. The facts can't be disputed. The Lord gathered the daughter of Israel from the field. A newborn. He raised her. He gave her everything. But that doesn't obligate her to internalize his perspective.

It's funny, but suddenly I don't feel the urgency, suddenly our time together doesn't feel limited. You no longer have to prove anything to me: not that you'll do whatever it takes to save me, not your concern for me – I can feel it, it needs no proof. You've been there for me more than enough, Ella, you've gone above

---

* "And when I passed by thee, and saw thee polluted in thine own blood, I said unto thee when thou wast in thy blood, Live; yea, I said unto thee when thou wast in thy blood, Live." – Ezekiel 16, 6, King James Bible.

and beyond. Don't worry about me. Don't worry about our relationship. The spaces that have opened up are helping me now, and I myself need time. I've shown you so many faces that I no longer know how to be with you, and I want to come to you with at least the facts sorted out. With my actions. With the things that happened to me. With the verdicts the world has ruled in my affairs.

A kiss and a hug,

Itamar

46

Itamar,

Something about your last email has left me without words. Maybe it was the very personal interpretation you made in "terms of endearment for you". Maybe the tender gratitude it conveyed. I know that even the emails that bubbled with fury embodied a love-hate quality, and yet, this one was different.

I therefore described where we stand to Sarah, my secret advisor on matters of caution, and on most other matters as well. Just so we're clear, she isn't reading your emails, but sometimes I tell her about the feelings they stir in me. One of the clearest conclusions I've reached after reading our friend Gabbard, is that right now I can't rely solely either on my judgment or yours. Our tendency towards shared confusion demands an external perspective. The French have a beautiful name for this particular state, "folie à deux," madness of two. Ever heard of it, Itamar?

In any event, Sarah easily identified the ways in which you minimize the magnitude of recent events while painting them in sexual hues, you like how I shower you with attention, it feels nice, as if I was merely coddling you a little, as if we're not dealing with matters of life and death. She especially pointed out the flirtatious description of kissing Jessica, the same woman you're charged with assaulting. You must admit, that's one clear-eyed sharp-tongued advisor I found for us.

Having set this clear, I wish to relate to the wonderful way you interpret biblical idioms for me. I've always enjoyed your ability to explain in everyday Hebrew ideas that are deeply rooted in our culture although somehow still remain foreign to me, but for you they are second nature. You write about the little daughter of Israel, the Lord's ragged waif, and I think to myself: strong words, Itamar, but does her rescue necessitate total subjugation? Is there a possibility for them, for us, to keep our true assets, to keep our perspectives and still join our thoughts?

Ella

47

What a morning.

Something's off. There was maintenance work on the subway, so I took the bus to the public library. You do know that I've already been authorized to leave the institution, right? I was racing to catch the bus, missed the curb and twisted my ankle. I chuckled in embarrassment and immediately put on a casual "nothing happened" kind of expression while limping on my aching ankle towards the back of the bus in search of an available seat. I sat down and laughed to myself. The way this mechanism works. The sense of humiliation and degradation doesn't even ask the brain permission to enter. I slip and fall, therefore I am, like some kind of Cartesian principle. A beautiful Puerto Rican smiled at me from the seat to my right. The sense of humiliation evaporated. Not at once, but slowly, by degrees. We are emotional machines, one smile gives me the courage to move forward.

The problem is that I simply can't stand the American light anymore. I'm dying to get out of here. It's as if the sun is wrapped in wax paper, and I can't see anything for what it is. I miss Israel's harsh yellow sun, the feeling that every object reflects its real color. Feinberg called yesterday. He wants to meet and talk about something. I'm almost sure he found out about the missing pages. I want to murder him. Sometimes I imagine myself shooting him, and then pointing the weapon at Jess and shooting her too. The next hearing is in two days. Keep your fingers crossed for me. And don't worry, I don't have a gun permit. Well, I know that isn't very reassuring when it comes from me, but what might reassure you is that I'm having fewer and fewer revenge fantasies.

I'm at the New York public library. Surrounded by quiet, obedient Americans. It's a spacious hall with long tables running the width of the floor, table after table, chairs, and reading lamps. I'm sitting and perusing a book about assault offenses written by an expert on criminal law. I feel like an ordinary member of the human race sitting here between a spindly old woman, bright eyed and wrinkled, and a young African American with a fashionable hat, and I shake my head at the thought. The stream of life is surging around me. But being in the public library of this liberated city, that represents the freest country in the world, and none the less has an "army" to protect "proper language", gives me a creeping sense of totalitarianism.

I'm looking at what I wrote. I am indeed consumed by hatred and rippled with aggression. I miss you, Ella. What are you doing right now? How does it feel to be back in Israel?

For a while there, during therapy, I thought to myself her empathy is real, she thinks about me outside therapy too. That's probably what happened in my last email. I suddenly believed you. Your insistence on visiting me, postponing your flight back to Israel, it really shook me. What can I say, your grand gesture made me believe everything else too, believe in you. That's where the tenderness came from.

I'm reading your last email again and finding that same shut-open-shut pattern. And I try to imagine how it would be to dive even deeper with you, open-open-open. And in the meantime I feel mostly sorrow. Throughout our entire correspondence, I never hated you. And no, I never thought of you as a sexual object. Aggression, yes, psychological projections, yes, but what human being doesn't fall for those traps? When I write about the body

I'm actually writing about the soul, and when I write about the soul I'm actually writing about the body, as you know. I'm writing about you.

Dear, wise Ella, I don't know if your friend Sarah is worthy of all your praise. She certainly helped me a lot behind the scenes. You don't need to apologize; what I write you is yours to do whatever you want with it. There's always a third party among us. And while you wish to stress its presence, I, just as adamantly, try to ignore it. So now you've summoned Sarah to be our third. But why are you trying to reassert her presence? I always chase my third away. I try not to listen to its criticism and ridicule. But what you wrote also inspired some hope: if you need a secret advisor on matters of caution, it means you're not being cautious, or at least not as you usually are. As in the Mishnah I am studying at the library: "One who says to one's peer 'I am forbidden by vow from you'; 'I am separate from you'; 'I am distanced from you'; 'I may not eat yours'; 'I may not taste yours.'" How much self-loathing must one feel to remove himself from his friend, to say he forbids himself to eat his friend's food. This vow becomes even more harsh towards the end of the chapter with the sacrificial term 'Konam': "Konam be my mouth which speaks with you, My hands which work for you, My feet which walk with you – he is forbidden."* Now even his body parts are out of reach, forbidden, his self-loathing is tearing him to pieces.

I'm trying to teach myself to look beyond the explicit, to think about what kind of depression drives a man to take such vows, about the people who thought it worthy to include such a thing

---

* "Konam" is a term used to express a vow since the later days of the 2nd temple (2nd century BCE). Literally it means "sacrifice", and it was used in the context of vows to indicate a distance taken from an object or a person as from a sacred sacrifice.

in a canonical text. And about you, Ella, about what draws you to such texts. Tell me something about it? Anyway, I hope Sarah realizes that the danger hovering above me isn't serious, it's like a speech balloon in a comic book: the words in the balloon can direct you towards the things, to state them or conceal them, but it's only in the drawing that you see them for what they actually are. It's pointless to look anywhere else. And Sarah will look at me, she'll see me beyond the words and the bureaucracy and the conversations with you, and understand that deep down, I'm a builder, not a destroyer.

Kisses and longing from New York. I thought I had time, we had time. Suddenly, in a split second, time is running out.

48

I'm spending the time on my flight going over our emails. I'm reading us like a novel, as a reader peering inside. Did you know that for the most part we write as if to ourselves? We don't make the effort to answer questions, we don't bother tying up loose ends. Were a stranger to read our correspondence, she couldn't help but wonder what was silenced between our words.

A long time ago, when I was very young, I broke up with my first love, the likes of whom I haven't met since. I remember walking along the buildings of the university, during a not-so-impressive Tel Aviv winter, still the wind whistling through the treetops, darkness descending, I'm wrapped in my coat feeling as lonely as could be, you get the picture... I remember imagining that inside my body there was a dark tunnel, and the wind was blowing through it. Oddly enough, that turbulent image calmed me down. With the wind blowing both inside and out, I imagined the tunnel filled with parts and pieces of our shattered love, lying between me and him. And I thought how we must each reclaim our own, sort the pieces and restore them to the body and soul that created them. It's not forgetting, it's not to disavow the link, but being so young I felt that otherwise there would be no separation. And that's why it hurts, I thought. Hurts like some reversed organ transplant, without painkillers or anesthetics.

Is that what we're avoiding, you and me? Never really separating, leaving our stuff hanging in the space between us? We sound so fixed in our ways; we write words that form rigid, repetitive patterns. And it's true there's a rhythm to it, just like you wrote: open-shut-open-shut, you-me-you-me stubborn agendas articulated in harsh words. If we don't recognize the influence, we don't have to acknowledge what the transition from therapy to our correspondence did to us, you don't have to avow your illness, me to avow my stay.

For the final words before I land, while in this exterritorial space between heaven and earth, I'll write that I am very sad. I'm leaving you in the American light, and in my Sarah and my Jeff's hands. Deep down, I don't believe my mother is dead. It doesn't make any sense to me, and I think maybe someone got the records mixed up. I keep hoping she'll be there when I land, and that maybe, finally, she'll be able to feed me with mother's milk instead of tears. Crocodile tears. Where does that expression even come from, crocodile tears?

We didn't talk about that long goodbye hug, about your attempt to kiss me, about the sudden burst of my murky tears. How can I explain that sometimes the important story is not the one found in the chaotic, crude strokes, or in the bold, cutting colors? Sometimes, the truly meaningful story is the one told quietly, with a few words, a slight nod and a gentle bat of an eyelid, in the fantasizing of a kiss. Not necessarily in the kiss itself.

49

I picture you, at home and sitting at your desk, reading what I wrote to you, thinking about our meeting, about the talks we had in therapy, and my eyes well up. All of a sudden my heart goes out to you. I hope you meet your mom when you go out for groceries, I hope she'll be there, and you feel her love for you.

It's also all the tension that has built up inside me. All the energy I spent, and suddenly we're somewhere else again, I see you clearly, you see me. How did that happen? How do these things happen? The moment you wrote that we're writing to ourselves, you breathed life into our shared existence, you created us with words.

Look at us: for you, with all your boundaries, all your down-to-earth wisdom, the line between reality and fantasy is so fluid. Whereas for me, who admitted to an inability to note a real distinction, there's a great, formidable wall standing between what actually happened and what could have been. And how could you of all people think that the story actually lies in the gentle bat of an eyelid, in the fantasizing of a kiss; how could you – who built, brick after brick, that same wall between reality and fantasy that I tried to tear down – write such a ludicrous thing. I wonder how much of this is you and how much your training in therapy. In your empathy, your desire to be there, with every fiber of your being, for each and every one of your patients. Where every piece of information he shares with you, whether a figment of the imagination or something grounded in reality, requires your sensitive response.

You know better than anyone how many years I've lived deterred by conventions, fearing what people might say. Whenever I crossed a line, I concocted theories by which one's Judaism manifests itself when one sins, because the sin in itself is Jewish. Now I realize how wrong I was. I feel alive when I work my body and mind together. It's deceptive at times, but nothing can replace that certainty or the liveliness that comes with it.

It is now that I feel you. Now I experience the world through emotions, and in my mind that airplane seat turns into a gushing, bubbling waterfall. Here come the tears. Your landscapes are so beautiful, so good.

I think we can never really separate. Even if you reclaim all those pieces of flesh and put them back where they belong, there will always be that part that's no longer the same, the spot where the lover has completely altered the cell's nucleus. You see, the cheek (and not the lips) you offered for my kiss was a bleeding piece of flesh. It tore me up inside. These are things we can't control, your cheek was acting on an internal decree and this incident will forever be part of us. For better or for worse. What were you crying about at that moment, Ella? The expression "crocodile tears" comes from the ancient belief that crocodiles weep in order to lure their prey. But I always imagined it quite differently, I see a lost crocodile, not knowing where he is, slithering through the mud, helpless and crying, crying because he doesn't really want to kill.

Itamar

50

Just for you, Itamar, an exhausted, addled email. I landed at 3:52 a.m. Have you ever noticed how people in the arrival areas of airports all have sallow, worn-out faces? We're all moving in a pack, march, stop, wait for passport control, resume marching. Luckily, we have our duty-free whisky and rustling bags of sweets, to remind us of our adventures in foreign lands. And while I march with such discipline and order, entirely alone and still duty-free, I grasped that she'll never be waiting for me, and that I will never be free of this "Waiting and waiting, crying and crying, for who has not come? Michael". And through the heavy tiredness, I imagined this annoying, symbolic Michael, who after all my waiting and crying still won't show his face. He's delaying because he himself is lost, stranded, and sobbing as he waits on one bank and I on another. There's probably some great Gemara portion on the subject of severance. Is it true that women aren't allowed to study Gemara? Why not? Were men terrified that women would come to their senses and leave?

Okay, I must try and focus. The jetlag, my mother's utterly inexplicable death, and the two of us – it's all tearing me up into small fuzzy pieces. I feel like diving into a soft bed, hiding under the covers, breathing in the fresh smell of linen, and never getting up. A kind of death mixed with hedonism, that's what I want, although I must be a normal mom now. What will I write to you, being normal? That you need to pull yourself together and settle your affairs in New York? That you need to be a man and come back to therapy? That you need to leave me alone? It's possible I'll want to delete this email from the curriculum vitae of our relationship. Very possible.

51

Ellonet,

Imagine a world in which there are no deletions. You can't delete anything, not in the Borgesian sense of a man who remembers everything, absolutely everything, but rather in the more legal sense – that every grain of sand remains as evidence, of your actions, your opinions, your crimes, your acts of kindness, jealousy, stinginess. This world, I believe, is the real one. My ongoing excommunication from human society has taught me that the persona we present to the world is totally unneeded. Even when you stand completely naked, exposing your former crimes and your present unacceptable behavior, even then people dress you in the clothes they choose for you. And that's the essence of the tale of "The Emperor's New Clothes": the people agreed to believe in the emperor's imaginary clothes not because they feared the repercussions of breaking the pretense, but because they feared his very nudity, feared looking at it, being around it.

Your brief emails, just like your colleagues' written texts, are a crying waste of energy spent on blurring the evidence. These are your emperor's new clothes, an invisible testament to your constant transgressions. You people distinguish between speech and writing, glorifying the written word. It doesn't surprise me that people who are supposed to be dealing with humanism in its deepest sense, placing the human being above all else, have actually succumbed to the postmodern position that strips the subject bare and rejects the superiority of Platonic idealism in favor of the written text.

What I'm asking, with all my heart, is that you write, Ella, write, but don't attribute such significance to the text. View it as a flexible trampoline that enables you to jump higher and higher without getting so tired. Because all these concealments, in both the spoken and written word, as well as in the avoidance itself, drain you. What does it mean "be a man and come back to therapy"? My damaged masculinity is slowly healing, but "be a man and come back to therapy" is an awful cliché. Just like you referring to what we had in therapy as "love" – a cliché stemming from an excess of either sarcasm or romanticism, I can't tell, because sometimes the two like to coexist.

In my next court hearing in two weeks, my lawyer, the one I met in the library, is still hoping they'll settle for community service, but you never know. Sometimes I feel like snatching Jess and making her disappear. I keep picturing her with Feinberg, fucking, watching me watching them, smiling, enjoying being watched by me. I visited Feinberg's office yesterday and took the rest of the manuscript, that idiot didn't even notice. Oh, and most importantly, right after that I saw Sarah on the street. She smiled at me, and we started talking. She really is great. We had a coffee together, spoke for at least an hour. She's older but her maturity is delightful, the way she takes her seat, the quiet calm she exudes, the ease with which she straightens her dress and holds her coffee cup. The most incredible thing is that I felt a sexual tension between us, something that rises from the body and permeates the conversation. Sarah is genuine. There's a wide gulf between how warmly you talk about her and the cool reserve she shows for you. Maybe it's because she doesn't want to reveal anything, maybe because she's a mother figure to you.

When going over your last email for a second time, I kept seeing the image of the little girl in the red coat from "Schindler's List" flashing before me. Tell me, how can you treat people while viewing the world as one big concentration camp? How do you do it? What does it do to you? Obviously, you see soldiers and barbed wire fences wherever you turn. And regarding your question – yes, you're not supposed to study the Gemara because of a man's deeply rooted fear of women. First and foremost, the fear that women will cohabit the religious arena, that they will be able to stand in the center of the synagogue, in the center of the place of Torah study, a horrible fear that they'll take over and exploit the texts for their lechery, their seduction. Some interpreted Rabi Eliezer's saying – "One who teaches his daughter Torah -- it is as though he teaches her frivolity" along those lines, the erotic, seductive interpretation. It's true, women now study everything, Torah, Mishnah, Talmud. But they're kept on a tight leash. When they study, they're not carrying out the mitzvah of Torah study like men. They're studying so they'll know how to conduct themselves in the world, how to observe the mitzvot, but not as an intellectual or spiritual venture that brings one closer to God. I too am afraid of you. Not of your intelligence, not of your sexy body, not in and of themselves. Like Rabi Eliezer, I'm concerned you'll use these things for evil; I'm not sure how good a person you are. I'm not at all sure how good women are. There's some twenty-first century progress for you, back to the primitive sensibility of the first century.

Go back to your therapy sessions, Ella. I'm no longer there, I've moved on. I'm not coming back to therapy. I'm someplace else. Alive. Kicking. Breathing.

I need money. For the third time, I need money. How much can you lend me? I promise to pay you back when I sell the pages I've sent you.

Itamar

52

My dear Itamar,

You should know I never really understood phrases like "the superiority of Platonic idealism". When I was a PhD student, I still made the effort to feign understanding, but I no longer have the desire to do so. You might find this surprising, but as a lecturer I do my best to avoid professional jargon of all kinds. I prefer simple words meant for real people. I understand, for instance, your words about that "flexible trampoline that enables you to jump higher and higher," and the erotic implication of bodies bouncing in some sweaty, unbridled revelry is not lost on me.

These past few days I've been feeling lighthearted on the verge of hypomania, if I may diagnose myself, and I know this too is related to my mother's death. She would have probably been horrified, but after a few dragging days and nights here, I started celebrating my alleged release from the heavy guilt I've carried my entire life. As if I've been invited to a very private cocktail party, and I'm meeting old friends I hadn't seen in ages: the effortlessness, the appetite, the indulgence of small comforts. Away with the solemn loneliness, the woeful grief, the weighty guilt. You see, I too can be dramatic.

When I wrote you about my mother's passing you responded with the sentence "I murdered my mother," and I was angry. But now, after The Thirty Days have passed, the tombstone unveiled, I'd like to express some genuine, though hypomanic, curiosity. Could it be true that no woman is of lighter limb than the woman unburdened by the weight of her mother? Nothing can be done to repair or further damage. That which has been stolen in the dead of night shall never be returned to its lawful owner.

I think the words "be a man and come back to therapy" referred to maturity and accountability rather than to masculinity, but I agree they may come across as something of a tease. I apologize for that. On that same note, please abandon the oedipal storyline with Sarah and me. Not all manipulations can work, and that nonsense you wrote about sexual tension between you two and the cold way she speaks about me just raised a sad smile to my face. I also can't send you money. Sarah will help you deal with the institutions, and if need be, she and Jeff will help you find affordable housing. When you return to Israel, I can provide therapy sessions for a symbolic fee. Stop laughing bitterly and just listen to us.

Enough, good night, my eyes are closing in front of the laptop. There is no need to fear me, I'm just a Little Red Riding Hood.

53

I have no idea what's going on with me.

The big things are getting mixed up with the little things. The world seems pointless. My hearing was yesterday. I decided to wait with my email so I could face you with the results. For better or for worse. Although I'm not that into you anymore—you're no longer my lighthouse, Ella—I still want you to like me, God knows why. What I had failed to achieve in years of therapy with you I've managed to pull off in a few months of letters. You've revealed yourself to me, all your weaknesses. And I don't like what I see. Not one bit. When you write to me about accountability and a "strange package," I know you're no longer treating me, and you never will. The judge looked at me and looked at Jess and Feinberg, rubbing their hands, waiting for me to fall. And still he gave me one more chance. He's making me meet a therapist once a week for two months. When the two months are up, he'll get a report, and if it satisfies him, he'll cancel the court order prohibiting me from leaving the country. So I immediately suggested Sarah as my therapist. I think she knew it was going to happen, she has experience with these kinds of cases. The judge was pleased. Apparently, Sarah is a pretty well-known figure around here. Now ask her why she agreed. Maybe you two aren't as tied as you thought? Maybe she's just being compassionate towards me, and maybe she finds this unity of yours a little difficult and just needs a little space.

I see you, Ella. And now my resistance surfaces: I hate when you repeat what I wrote just to mock me. Who even copies someone else's words? Someone who can't reflect, who doesn't want to understand, who rejects everything. I hate that you feel the need to mention your PhD, or the fact that you're a lecturer. What good does it do? What, the PhD has become part of your body? Did you give birth to it like you gave birth to the girls? All these birth metaphors are so clunky and hollow, they portray a vast insecurity.

Only the issue of the money continues to be a source of pain. I was held up in some shabby, stinking sublet until Sarah offered me a room in their house for the next two months, and I jumped at the opportunity. Go figure. In warm, Middle Eastern Israel therapists are standoffish and conservative, whereas here, in the cradle of Puritan culture, people take risks. Maybe she sees me as some kind of startup, a case study or a springboard for her or Jeff's next book. Anyway, I'm taking them up on their offer and will soon leave this shithole for Sarah's pleasant pastures. It'll be interesting to be with people, share a kitchen with them, a bathroom. Share a space. Although I bet they have separate bathrooms, god forbid they should get under each other's feet. Just thinking about it makes my skin crawl. I've gotten so used to being on my own, alone between four walls, and even though these walls kept colliding they were still my personal, albeit tremorous, space.

Here's something for you, Ella, so you'll feel like you've gained something from my letter, that you haven't read this far for nothing: according to Halakha, a man is forbidden to build a wall within a distance of four cubits from his friend's wall. Interesting, right? But alongside the interdiction there is also the urge, the need to break down that barrier. How did those genius assholes come up with the forbiddance to sit within four cubits of the outcast? But I'm no longer an outcast. Jeff is coming to get me soon. When he places his hand on my shoulder, I can feel the weight of his compassion. Karma works in mysterious ways, maybe the whole purpose of our relationship was for me to meet Sarah and Jeff, for her to come to my aid and for me to have a temporary but real home after such a long period of vagrancy.

By the way, I'm almost sure Jess is pregnant. There wasn't an ounce of fat on her, and now her belly is round and puckered. She and Feinberg are an item. She looks good, even great, and it worked in my favor – she certainly wasn't scarred. How psychotic is it to want to kill the person who's the reason I'm on trial? To see her carrying in her womb the child of someone who never treated me like a human being, someone who wants to exact his revenge on me because I was inside his lover before him? Any reasonable person would see that Feinberg is just jealous of me because I knew how to handle her exactly like she needs to be handled, violently. In court, what I saw in Jess's eyes wasn't fear of me, nor was it a desire for revenge. It was something much scarier. I saw a desire to make me disappear. To erase me while the little Feinberg grows inside her. She took such pleasure in our locking gaze.

I can feel the force of life draining from my body. Now, of all times, when I'm being ferried into Sarah and Jeff's home. Now, of all times, when life is reemerging. I pinned everything on that trial, on the verdict, and without it the idea of carrying on seems unthinkable. Meaningless. Yes or no to lifting the toilet seat, yes or no to killing myself, to shaving, to going out for cigarettes, is it worth it or not. I'm confused by the passage of time, love won't save me, buying bread for dinner, it's all mixing and melting and filling my mouth with dirt. It's as if once the judge gave his verdict a giant cement mixer was turned on and my life now depends on the arbitrary decision of a construction site manager.

Itamar

54

I'm in an odd position, Itamar, sitting quietly by my desk in the office, yet writing from within a rumbling earthquake, which no one else seems to feel but me. Still, something was ripped apart, forcefully thrown into the distance, and the stifling dust has not yet settled, can you see?

I've been thinking a lot about my part in our correspondence, trying to figure out the hidden motives that were in play. It's clear that there was something I needed from you, desperately needed. After all, this entire correspondence could have been stopped straight away, right after your first turbulent email, and obviously I didn't want to stop, not really, not until the end. I told a friend here of this correspondence, then mentioned it to a colleague, both were terrified to learn that I had turned you into my addressee. They talked about the risk on my part, my naiveté, and foolishness. What was that thing, I saw them pondering with inquisitive eyes, that I wanted so badly that I was willing to lose perspective like that, to dive into a freefall?

I could tell them of my obvious rescue fantasies, that stubborn perpetual idea that I could find you, maybe even reach this inner place from which life seems worth living. But truth be told, it has a lot to do with your own persistent beliefs that I can be reached and truly be touched. Your piercing receptors were always attuned, trying to figure me out, to find me between my lines. How voraciously and shrewdly you tried to parse my thoughts, my desires, my delusions... And whether you were right or wrong, and whether you considered me through your eyes or mine, and even if you merely wrote to yourself through me, I was always on your mind.

I could tell them of long forgotten gentle words, of thought-provoking striking questions, of verbal magic tricks so skillfully performed just for me. I could try and describe how bright ideas gradually submerge into a swamp of confusion, and how I never know when we will sink again, so I perpetually guard the castle.

I could tell them of your cruelty. The sophistication by which you examine foreign territory, then invade it and take over, make it yours. Your inexplicable freedom to reach out and grab, crudely, powerfully, terribly. And strangely enough, this liberty you allow yourself is unbearable and yet elicits something else in me, something I find difficult to articulate yet ostensibly present, could this be what I needed to learn from you?

But as I try to be stripped of all veils, completely attuned to my own wishes, I don't want to love you nor hate you, not to pretend, not to listen, not to breathe in the toxic fumes of your thoughts. I don't want to run wild with anger, I don't want to be robbed blind anymore. Itamar, I asked Sarah to take you under her wing, you must know that, so what kind of twisted triangular structure were you attempting to design between us? Who were you trying to hurt, through the seducing and inveigling of whom? Did you even think your plan through? Because even though you know almost nothing about the gift I gave you by bringing you to my Sarah and Jeff, you can no doubt grasp with those sensitive receptors of yours that it's my secret garden. Wasn't the invitation enough? Did you have to barge in and plunder?

There, you've come upon my border, welcome to the transit terminal. It's not easy to reach my border, many times it keeps moving, stretching as if it has a life of its own. I'm so trained at swallowing and digesting the materials of others, as if programmed to drink bitter, dark milk. Yet from where I stand now, it seems possible to say: don't mock my limitations. Don't steal more than I was willing to give.

Regarding your question about psychosis, the answer is loud and clear: yes, Itamar, the inability to distinguish where you end and the other begins, the other's body, the other's psyche, feeling that it's all blended and blurred, that is psychotic. To mourn the distinction but agree to preserve it, that's neurotic. True, it may be disappointing at times, but most of us do our best to live with it.

As to your misconceptions about what happened in the court-house and the matters of Jess's pregnancy and Freud's-secret-sto-len-texts, I'll leave it to you and Sarah. I'm assuming that by now you've already met your probation officer and joined the therapy group, and that all these people have made you aware of your court-appointed community service and living arrangements. I will retreat now, this separation has been long due, but I finally accept it.

Ella

Part 2
"In Thy Blood, Live"

55

Itamar,

Have you ever heard of Andrew McAuley? A strange opening indeed, but I've been thinking a lot about his adventure lately, mostly in relation to you and me. Anyhow, Andrew wanted to be the first person to cross the Tasman Sea by kayak. To ford the 1,600 kilometers between Australia and New Zealand, he would have to spend at least one month alone at sea. So Andrew practiced paddling and rowing, equipped his kayak with food and water as well as a camera and a satellite phone, and set off. Like a complete fool. The Tasman Sea is often hit by powerful storms, with waves ten and even twelve meters high to jolt Andrew inside his flimsy little shell.

There are heartrending shots of him leaving for his first attempt: his wife embracing his limber body and not letting go, their toddler calling out excitedly, "Goodbye, Daddy!" and Andrew rowing away from them with his strong arms, and suddenly starting to cry. He left on his second attempt only a month later, his body wrapped in a yellow windbreaker, his face painted in a thick coat of sunblock that lent him the appearance of a swaying corpse. The shots of dark dense waves enveloping him drew me in with a lamenting whisper, I can't get them out of my mind.

Sarah visited me in Tel Aviv after more than a year, bringing with her a surge of memories. For months I didn't ask, and she respected it, until a sharp thin layer of ice covered all that had happened. But this afternoon I've learnt so many things: that my last email surprised you, that at first you seemed to be mourning but after a while you started seeing your social worker regularly and met with the therapy group too. You found a little place in Brooklyn, not far from the basement you hid in. I learnt that at the second court hearing, Feinberg stated that at the time of Jessica's assault you were amid an acute psychotic episode, and Sarah corroborated his statement with an optimistic evaluation of your psychiatric prognosis. The team that treated you noted your cooperation and remorse. You got six months of community service. Jessica wasn't pregnant.

I feel the silly need to repeat Sarah's words, as if it could eliminate the elusive triangular quality that was thriving near the end of our correspondence. You should know I was smiling when I heard you and Jeff developed the habit of meeting in the park near the beautiful library, to talk about the books you had read. Then, after the community service ended, you stayed around to tie up a few loose ends and bid everyone a warm farewell. You are in Tel-Aviv for over a month now, Sarah said.

I listened carefully from within my tiny kayak. While I was rowing and rowing seas retreated, continents moved, straits narrowed down. Andrew was only thirty-five kilometers from his finish line, when his muffled distress signal was received on the shores of New Zealand, but he was never found. What was his expedition for? What good did it bring to the world? What good did I bring, so often miscalculating direction and distance, letting my longings divert me from my route? I'm rowing and rowing, as far as I can from you, straight into your heart, and I'm not moving at all.

I would like to say goodbye face to face.

Ella

56

Dear Ella,

It felt strange to hear from you after all this time.

Strangely nice actually.

Like a clock whose hands had come to a halt, and suddenly, without warning, time awoke from its frozen slumber, and they started turning again. Because while many things had happened, we both moved on, each with our own means of transportation and landscape spreading out before us. **Our** time came to a standstill with the last email you sent, and now it's starting to move again. I can feel it. If I had to choose an image, to match your kayak, I'd say I was driving a steam locomotive snaking between mountains and valleys. My path is not an easy one and my destination is unknown, but it's a beautiful ride. I wake up every day to the trains whistle, to the faces of the passengers who accept my presence and greet me with a nod, and I ride on. I think about Andrew, meaning you, at sea, rowing with one hand in my direction and with the other away from me, the waves rage and the continents move, and that thought is, at the very least, disturbing. I have a vague and frustrating memory of being pulled in opposite directions. Being neither here nor there, stuck.

I would love to meet with you, I just have to ask Naomi if it's okay with her, she's heard so much about you and knows how complicated it is. I'll let you know as soon as possible.

I have no desire to contest even a single fact you mentioned about last year's events. If they taught me anything, it's that acceptance and intimacy have nothing to do with creating a shared narrative, but with something much more fundamental, and more level, albeit obscure. Because when I read your letter, your account of my past year felt more like a hidden desire to make sure Sarah was telling you the truth, and it's for that reason alone you wanted to eliminate the "elusive triangular quality." I'm laughing out loud now. Remember how I criticized you for repeating things I said? And here I am now, doing the exact same thing. Something remains from every relationship. Maybe that is what I took from you, the grace of mulling over someone else's words.

I remember your concerns about my relationship with Sarah. The moment I recognized them, I tried to compound your anxiety. It's my survival reflex. I'm sorry. In a way, it worked. In fact, it worked so well that you decided to end our relationship. You spoke of boundaries and severed the entire web of intricate ties between us all at once. I really didn't understand it back then. I understand it better now. I guess that what you've built with her is like your nuclear reactor. And whoever attacks it is doomed. My cooperation with ending our relationship, as difficult as it was, didn't stem from my desire to avoid a world war, but from the understanding that I needed a different kind of energy. Not the energy that swirled between us. You know those tired clichés about being generous with love, and how only love creates more love, they tend to bring out of me a bitter smile at best. As irritating as it can be, I realized that is exactly what I needed. Someone who knows how to volunteer love, without the need to portion it out or the fear of the triangle eating into her supply. I am less of a cynic than I thought. Clichés are my middle name nowadays. Sarah helped me a lot. You're welcome to ask anything regarding our relationship, I promise to answer fully and candidly. During the month I stayed at Jeff and Sarah's, they didn't mention you, for better or for worse. They created a separation that was good for me. For all of us, I guess. What's painfully beautiful is that I actually thought that if I never spoke to you again, I could break the triangle. Maybe Sarah thought so as well, if she didn't mention your name, the acute angles would cease to exist. I guess that that's the nature of self-deception, is it not? We seem to master it. With that in mind, our break wasn't a real separation either. In all truth, I didn't let go and I still don't fully grasp the gap between what I thought would happen and what happened in reality. I still haven't figured you out. I still want to.

Naomi. You wouldn't believe how long it took her to convince me of the sincerity of her intentions. She used every maneuver possible, including the physical ones unavailable to you as a therapist. She showed up at the most unexpected and inappropriate times. As unexpected as it was, I showed up as well. I was really there and could see her for who she is.

Nufar and Tamir, our neighbor's kids, just popped by for a visit, and I promised to show them a funny YouTube video of Americans reactions to Israeli snacks for the first time. Write me again? I'll talk to Naomi.

Itamar

57

Itamar,

I don't know why your kindest words cut into me. Horrible little cluster bombs. Of course it's fine that you ask Naomi, but it will have to be soon. We are on borrowed time.

Ella

58

Ella,

What do you mean by borrowed time?

59

I'll try to explain, but first, it's important to note I could sense through your writing that you're doing better. It seems that you've raised yourself out of the dark pit you were in just a year ago, and that's wonderful. Well done!

When I wrote that your words feel like cluster bombs, the sort that contain tiny projectiles scattered in every direction, I referred, perhaps not so elegantly, to the insinuation of the slightest offenses which later wreak havoc all over. Like that casual remark about the "month I stayed at Jeff and Sarah's," which I know isn't true, yet so skillfully resurrects the triangular quality I was hoping to tone down. Maybe your words are more of a precision-guided munition, aimed directly at me, accurate as hell. Which might explain why I'm getting too emotional too fast, without a shred of elegance left.

Let me then tell you something that is true. I've known Sarah and Jeff since I was very young, about nineteen. I was discharged in the middle of my military service, when I was diagnosed with an autoimmune disease, one of the nastier ones. I guess no illness is more fitting for me than an internal attack well-navigated by au courant intelligence, and maybe that's why nothing helped for so long. There were absurd amounts of medications, prolonged hospitalizations followed with my mother weeping at my bedside, yet the prognosis remained unclear. Everything that followed, everything you derided me for achieving in my life, it wasn't at all obvious that I could.

At the time, I was certainly not ready to surrender. Amid the chaos, I announced I was leaving to travel the world. I had this trip mapped out in my head, it included Rome, Copenhagen, Tokyo, Shanghai. My parents were mortified, they enlisted a whole battalion of threatening doctors, my mother cried her eyes out, but I insisted on going. As I limped my way to buy the plane ticket, we reached a compromise: I would modify my journey to include several stopovers at selected acquaintances of my parents, who would make sure that I get blood tests done and regulate my medications. Sarah, whom I hadn't met back then but knew she was a doctor, was granted veto rights concerning rehospitalization abroad. And so I set out on my adventure.

You can probably imagine how the time I had spent in New York with Sarah and Jeff changed everything. Although physically I was free falling, they had numerous healing gifts for me, from the look in their eyes as they listened, to their beloved books they so cleverly introduced to me, one by one. Whenever she had free time, Sarah would sit with me for hours, daydreaming my future together, asking good questions, laughing and goofing off, then sobbing but not crocodile tears. Never, in my entire life, had I experienced such wholesome love.

Can you understand it was then that I decided I would be a psychologist? It was as if my childhood Lisa, who was actually Lottie, drowning in their father's living room, suddenly knew that tears could have a recipient, the right one. It was then that I came upon the very personal idea, that I too would like to convert bitter milk into words that give nourishment. And perhaps you could also understand why I brought you to Sarah and Jeff when you lost your mind, knowing without even realizing it, that through them you would know how similar we are.

It was a difficult year, Itamar. My mother's death sent me back to the skim, lonely milk of my beginnings. The exhausting mind games with you were simply the final nail in the coffin. I was failing, I gave all that I had but it wasn't enough. Then I tried for a while to be Andrew, hoping that an utter and complete acceptance of my solitude would help me comprehend what was fundamentally damaged. But I wasn't that good at abstinence either.

Which finally brings me to the borrowed time. Mind the fucked-up symbolism, my Andrew year has ended with a stormy reappearance of my autoimmune disease, which had been sluggish enough to let me ignore it for quite some time. I wish I knew the hidden message this relentless internal intelligence insists that I hear. The little cluster bombs are the manifestations of my envy. I just don't seem to do life right.

Next week I'm flying to Basel, for an experimental treatment that might slow things down. How I wish I could go instead to Rome, Copenhagen, Tokyo, or Shanghai! Since I don't know exactly when and in what state I'll return, the reasonable thing was to close my practice, at least for now. The reasonable unacceptable thing. This is what I've been up to the past few weeks, and I'd like to say goodbye to you too.

Ella

60

Ella,

Who are you going with? Who's accompanying you? Who's taking care of you during your treatments? I'll come, if you let me. I can also be fun, you know, I could keep you company. I could finally see you at the airport sitting with your feet up, observing everyone around while drinking your coffee, your hands hovering above the sandwich your mother never made you. Just say yes, there's a couple of things I wanted to buy at the duty-free anyway. For years I've been wanting to try out that sentence, which to me represents the most normal version of normal, and for years I found it so loathsome, and now I've just been waiting for those words to roll off my tongue, or at least write them to you. See? Lucky you got cancer... :)

You are accurate. So exact. Each of your words stems from the core, and yet, I find it hard to reply, hard to describe things as they are. This time, crazy Hebrew is to blame, it's a language that turns everything that's real into the processed and edited version of us, as if the world really was created by the twenty-two letters of the Hebrew alphabet and there's no distinction between the world, the body, and the soul. That Kabbalistic mumbo-jumbo, that God compressed himself and into that empty space that remained, entered the most basic elements of creation, the letters...it makes sense to me now. You, me, us... such sublime and miserable creatures. And maybe that type of connection between the words and the world is reserved solely for those facing death, with the end staring them in the face, touching them, embracing them with caressing, clutching arms. And it is thanks to you that I can see it. Suddenly the body, the soul, our minds are speaking in one voice, loud and clear. I read you, feel you, I know that now, you are real. But you challenge reality, proclaim that you are unprepared, reluctant. If you are a page resting on a page, then there's no space or distinction between them. If you're a flower, the petals are whole, unblemished.

You once asked me if I could imagine how you decided to become a therapist. The answer is yes. I absolutely can, but in a different way. The cancer wants me to make allowances for you. Leave certain things for later. But there aren't any allowances between us, there never were. You have cancer, right? Please call the disease by its name, otherwise it remains an undefeatable monster.

And you will defeat it. You must. Take it, slam it against every possible wall, summon all the darkness inside you for this. You must, Ella. Do you hear me?

I am returning to what you wrote me, that the fountainhead from which your therapeutic approach issues is the relation between adoption and parenting. Because not all breast milk is good, and parenting is not a biological matter but an emotional one that has to do with love. And as such, therapy too is a form of adoption, the ability to trade, even for a short period, the biological system for a more fitting one. Because maternal biology fails so often, it fumbles, damages, even kills. There's so much beauty in what you wrote. So much grace. But I don't believe in it. You can't place blood and grace in the same category. Even an unloving father, a difficult, abusive father, is more of a father than an adoptive parent will ever be. A bad father is still a father. No, Ella, when we say "father," or call out to our mother, we are not talking about the roles of caretaking, love or responsibility.

That's a cultural and psychological construct, designed to deal with the bitter fact that so many parents simply fail in these roles that are supposed to be "natural." But when we say mother or father, we mean a pool of genes, blood, hormones that connect us to those we descend from. Whether we're in an infinite separation process from them (mother) or an infinite process of drawing closer to them (father). And that's why breast milk will always be irreplaceable. Always. I believe wholeheartedly that a person whose mother or father failed to care for him will not be able to tend to others. That parental care is the Archimedean point from which care and therapy originate. Very few, perhaps one in every generation, are born with such a strong, innate inclination that all the abuse, apathy and wickedness cannot diminish its power. That's why I was astounded when Naomi told me she wanted to adopt a child. Suddenly I'm panicking, because there's something very fundamental about this world that I don't understand, and I ask myself what that says about us, Naomi and me, and what will happen to us. Have I upset you, Ella?

Neither good milk nor poisoned milk – your therapy is not breastfeeding. Your therapy is medicine. Smart medicine, that is based on worldly wisdom and science, and sometimes it's only that medicine that stands between the patient and the bitter end.

You knew what medication I needed, and you wrote me prescriptions. Then you took notes, tried to understand me, to understand yourself. And I, who had already drunk from the breast milk and then drank some more, needed to put myself in the hands of someone who could diagnose me and give me what I required in order to pull myself together. And if you had any doubt as to who is the greater, more courageous hero, know that it is you – you are the true hero. You're one of those rare, probing therapists, who truly seek to learn and find out what happened. Even if you really wanted to be, you're not one of those whose breast milk replenishes time and again merely by conducting the session. I still think that all of you, psychologists and psychiatrists of all types, are very dangerous, don't get me wrong (now you're laughing, admit it). But as far as the treatment you people offer, those are separate planets. Dangerous, but separate. I have no idea if what I'm writing you now will encourage or offend, and my insensitivity is all too known to you, but you don't need to worry about losing your therapeutic energies. They will run out only when you come to understand who you are. And you yourself said you are not there yet.

Your abstinence has exhausted you. Of course it has. Sometimes people just need someone. And I'm here for you. It's not only my duty to be here for you as you were there for me, out of reciprocity or decency. No. It's also something I want. When I told Naomi about our relationship, she held my hands and said: "Bless that woman, bless that woman who knew how to get you across the ocean. To me." I'm a romantic, I still think love is salvation, but you of all people don't have to be a suicidal romantic, lost between the crushing waves. Your soulmate isn't the one who will save you, but the one who will anchor you. And that soul can be found anywhere, even in a treatment room in Switzerland.

Your Andrew was a scientist of the body and the soul, and he started out by testing his theory on himself. When I observe him setting out on his voyage, I realize his noble act. While his decision to set sail might seem deranged to some, to me it makes perfect sense. There were days I thought I was still capable of such acts, remember? It's funny how you were the one who tried to talk me out of them in a thousand and one ways, with endless prescriptions for the soul, day in and day out. Whereas now it turns out you are the one who's so close to it, seeking a path to the sea. Life is full of surprises.

Naomi is yelling from the other room that she has found my passport. I'm waiting to hear from you.

Itamar

61

My dearest Itamar,

I've made such a mess of everything. I should have never taken such liberty to express my thoughts and feelings, I'm so sorry. This is not an excuse for rowing carelessly, but it has been very emotional for me to conduct my goodbye meetings with patients, and I'm not at my best. I'm truly sorry.

I'm going to Basel on my own Itamar, no doubt about that, but I did want some closure with you, and a better understanding of where we stand. I get how cancer fits the puzzle, but I have an autoimmune disease with a rather stubborn and dramatic personality, and I'm not writing its name, so you won't become a sudden expert on it. I assume I'll survive, I'm just not sure how. I mean, I don't know what kind of quality of life I will have, and in case we meet soon you might notice limitations in movement and vision, but I'm still me. Not the best version, but me. You see, this isn't some scene out of "Love Story" left on the editing floor.

And I really don't think I'm a researcher-therapist and that I gave you smart medicine, certainly not prescriptions issued from a distant computer terminal. And parenting, in all its modes and forms, is about the willingness to stay awake for them, to shine a flashlight into the darkness under all the beds in the world, to wish them opportunities, to sometimes hate them for their opportunities but still enable them, until our last breath. What a mess. And I can't calm it down now, I simply can't.

Ella

62

I am with you.

I am with you for the mundane errands. To look into something, to buy something in the grocery store, or just to laugh or talk. Not because you rowed in my direction or because you lost direction, but because I feel you know where you came from and where you're heading. In any event, I'm here. Not because you cried out for help but because I'm a person in your life – not in the first or second circle, but still within the range of your life.

I must have done something right in my last email, because yours is full of resistance, and maybe that's the source of your refusal to reveal yourself to me, in or outside of therapy, to stand and say: I'm weak. The moment you admit it, something will collapse and disappear. One brick in the wall of resistance will come loose, and after that – what? Because that's the foundation of our relationship, it works best when you feel you have to put up walls, resisting something in the world, going against your parents or parental figures, against patients, against your girls, against life, against death. And then, who would have thought, you call on me, me of all people, with my ability to irritate you. In front of me you turn into some kind of sophisticated construction company, not only building dams and fortifications, but also bridges and escape tunnels. Ella, put down your shovels, your hoes, and picks. I am here for you. If you suddenly change your mind and want me there beside you, I'll come. If you get bored, call. If a thought just happens to pop into your head or you want to hear my annoying voice, don't think twice.

This time of year used to be a period of soul-searching for me, to reflect on the road taken, to repent. "That a sinner should abandon his sins and remove them from his thoughts, resolving in his heart, never to commit them again," as Maimonides writes in The Laws of Repentance. But now I seldom feel remorse for an act I committed, as if my conscience has dulled, everything has turned grayer, less sharp, or maybe I just like myself more. That's what Naomi says, my goodhearted Numi, but I suspect she only wishes to assuage me, so I won't falter again, won't throw myself into a tailspin, we already had one of those this year.

Some artists have managed to provide solace for an entire generation of readers through the mere act of self-exposure, of picking through their lives and rummaging through their souls, just as Andrew wanted to do. I believe he set out to sea in order to disprove the Greek tragedies, to show that after all, man can overcome the forces of nature, that fate isn't malevolent, that man can cope, decide, determine. The only question that remains is whether Andrew losing the battle worsened or improved the human condition. Is there some elaborate game in which we have just lost a point? Or maybe we scored an unintended own goal in some modern oedipal maneuver. Or maybe I'm just reverting to clichés again, viewing his resistance, the moment his kayak touched the water, as the moment he fulfilled his humanity, defying the world to which he had been banished.

It is the lot of all humans to turn a blind eye to our animalistic nature, to the fact that we are organic matter like animals, living, slowly rotting, dying. And maybe that's what makes people wash their hands of biological parenting and exalt adoption. It's not Naomi's motivation. She wants kids more than any woman I have ever met, with a kind of natural and pure desire, they don't necessarily have to be hers biologically, but just kids who need us as much as we need them. She really is a selfless person. Not like me. Or you. I look at her beautiful breasts when she gets dressed and undressed. Does that embarrass you, Ella? And yet, I write and I don't delete. I look at her, and as far as I'm concerned, breasts can breastfeed. Point blank. That's the main thing. Neither the relationship nor the worry nor the responsibility have anything to do with it.

Naomi wants to meet you.

Itamar

63

Itamar, you don't hear a word I'm saying, and I can't stand this anymore. The walls are long shattered, the construction company closed down, haven't you noticed? And it is scary, I get it, I should have never written such awful words to you, but I can't take in the pretentious mumbo-jumbo you're sending.

So stop thumping your bible at me, as if you are a rabbi. I will not meet your rebbetzin. And I truly hated the disgusting "lucky you got cancer" with that stupid smiley, no less.

64

Is that what you want? To dump on me everything the disease brings with it? Your inability to find a relationship? I almost turned the other cheek, so used to the punches of others, how Christian of me. I enjoy the attention so much that I almost fail to notice the poisoned arrows you're shooting at me. It's ironic that this insight is the product of an afternoon spent in your office a long time ago. You sat in your armchair, cross-legged, unattainable, and all of a sudden I deciphered that mechanism that made me put up with every punch. It was only then that I stopped with that "they called me so I came," with that passive Itamar, my default mode until that moment.

How did we get back to the equation I myself came up with a little over a year ago? How come the waves pushing us apart and pulling us together are so high, confused, conflicted? We seem to move forward, perfectly in sync, but end up back at square one, where your welfare depends on my self-hatred, my disappointment. Not only mine, of all your patients. It's not only hard cash that exchanges hands, from patient to therapist – the bread you eat is the bread of affliction, the clothes you wear are sewn from the grief of others. It's the economy of the soul. All the masks in the world won't hide your wrath when a patient dares to feel good about himself, to recover on his own.

My body aches when I think about your illness. I didn't offer to join you because I felt sorry for you, or guilty. It was as if your email triggered something, awakened the dormant connection between us.

Ella, I'm not a rabbi, I didn't find God, I only found Naomi. My Numi with her kind almond eyes, and her little fingers, and her good, healing, embracing hug. And somehow my life is more tolerable. On your couch, I always connected relationships to conservatism, to religiosity, and now it all erupts like some computers worm I had planted, and the unwitting worm is gnawing at me again. I'm looking up from the computer to see what Naomi is doing and where she is, as if I've cheated on her merely by thinking such a thing, and she, carefree, is singing Idan Raichel, "and then everything touches me, all the wonders of the day," and I feel a twinge in my heart. And when I quoted Maimonides I was abiding by your request, you immortal goddess, who repeatedly stated how much you enjoy it when I quote scripture. But like the biblical God, you too are capricious and uninhibited and unstable, unleashing a flood when you can't contain your fury. So die, Ella. Amen. You mercurial goddess, be banned from Olympus and become a mere mortal, you and all your abusive researcher-therapists.

What have I done to deserve this? Offered help? Acted like a human being? That thing I crave, your validation that I'm human, normal, that I have the capacity for understanding, compassion, empathy—that, you will never give me. That's my punishment for daring to break free from you, and now, how unbelievably awful, you're even using your illness to hurt me. You're reproaching me for making light of your cancer. What do you think I was trying to do? Get a laugh out of you with a narcissistic remark? A little lightheartedness. And almost immediately you used that gesture against me. How did I fail to notice, during all those long sessions, how dangerous you are to me? Naomi would have probably stopped me now, would have defended you, but she's not here to instill love in me, to make me a better person. With each kiss she softens me, brings me closer to a lush, bountiful, natural, pleasant earth. And that's what drives you mad, turns you into a wild beast.

The truly terrible thing is that I'm still playing this game with you, and by doing so, I'm pushing her away. Despicable.

I'm taking a deep breath. Trying to clear my mind of thoughts. Session after session and nothing has changed. I'm like a coil waiting to be sprung, but there's also life. People. There's you. And you're sick. And I ask, myself if not you, how to maintain the relationship between us, between two people who can't stand each other, and how to help you cope. These two questions are butting heads, refusing to accept that they are one question. Please, Ella, help me out here. Tell me where you want me, how I can help, how to talk to you, where it is that I do you good, make you laugh, fascinate you, if there is such a place.

I myself keep saying that what we have between us is a relationship, that a relationship is a relationship is a relationship, and the entire issue of boundaries is nonsense, a virtual line that keeps getting crossed, time and again. In a relationship you have to be willing to get hurt. As I read your email, a faded memory suddenly flickered before me – my dad hugged me yesterday. Yes, that hard man took me into his arms. Suddenly I realized, physically, the connection between fatherhood and worry; like an electrical circuit coming to life, I was charged with millions of watts. So worry indeed, towers above biology.

You were right.

And when it is missing, we become abandoned, derelict power stations, out in the wilderness.

And maybe that's the answer when it comes to blood. To the father. The mother. The brother. Sister. To start again with a hug, a kiss, any kind of touch.

And for us, what is that thing?

65

Itamari,

I'm leaving tomorrow. How I wish I could make all this go away with me. You should know that underneath my private desperations and jealousies, I remember well how you sounded just a few weeks ago, and I hope you would keep looking for this kind of being. Your relationship with Naomi must have a wonderful stabilizing effect on your being. It's a beautiful name – Naomi, always makes me hum that heartfelt song by Ralph McTell[*], in which Naomi "keeps a gentle edge" on him... My parents used to listen to this record again and again: "She wasn't all I wanted, but she's all I'll ever need", and I knew it was about grownups' tender love.

But you call her Numi, right? like in this old Hebrew lullaby, "Numi, numi yaldati[**]" Sleep, sleep, my little girl, "Numi, numi, nim". Soft tune with awful words, as in so many lullabies, do you remember? "Sleep, sleep, my little one, daddy's gone to work, he'll return when the moon comes out...Daddy went to the vineyards, he'll return when the stars come out". Daddy went to the orchard, then to the field, such a busy man indeed.

I once met a psychologist, a very impressive and truly charming man, who in his old age sought therapy from none other than a former patient. He told me that he felt this former patient was the only psychologist he could trust with his heart. What do

---

[*] https://www.youtube.com/watch?v=pBjl6voVQ_I&ab_channel=fritz51304

[**] "Sleep, Sleep" – a Hebrew lullaby by Yehiel Halperin, translated by Merav Menachem.

you think about that? He gave his former patient a precious gift, I know, but at the same time he also took something invaluable from him. And there are no "refunds" here, no cancellations, no going back... So even though recently a lot has happened in my life to sidetrack me, that's no reason to rob you of your psychologist and hand you a confused, needy, tempestuous woman in her place.

I guess I've never known the right distance with you: close, but not too much, apart, but not too far away. Keeping this in mind, I feel it would be fair to let you know I will not be traveling alone after all. Your writing actually helped me understand how idiotic and even moralistic this would be. I already can't see very well, and one of my legs has stopped fulfilling the role we had agreed upon forty years ago, an unfortunate combination which makes me stumble. I'll go with my friend Uli. When Uli needs to return to Israel, our friend Nina will replace her.

You know, when I read, I must enlarge the font to an ungodly size, until your emails appear as giant word after word, long strings of partial objects. And during the treatment in Basel, it will probably be worse for a while. What would you write if you knew that Uli and Nina read your words aloud to me? Would you use the same words? It will do us good to let others in on our secret. Naomi. Uli. Nina. The board of psychologists. The lords of psychoanalysis. The Swiss police.

66

It's hard for me to imagine you in this condition. Are you in pain? I hope not. I pretend you're not suffering and continue to write.

Of course I would use the same words, the same words in the same exact order. What difference does it make who reads you my letters? I've laid all my cards on the table. But what do I know about you? You, who treats everything like a deep dark secret. I know about your problematic relationship with your mother, I know you've never had a long, serious relationship with a man aside from the father of your daughters, but other than that I don't know anything about you. Who's Uli? Who's Nina? I don't even want to know anymore, don't tell me. And now, when you have so little to lose, you're still engaged in manipulations, calculating moves, scared I'll write something Uli or Nina might read and be horrified by. I really don't understand, why don't you just let it all hang out for once? Fuck the board of psychologists, and besides, I've never heard of a law forbidding a patient to maintain a relationship with a former psychologist, these are all your made-up rules to make sure that heaven forbid, heaven forbid... What are you so afraid of?

Ella, you haven't been my psychologist for a long, long time, and I haven't treated you as such since the very first time I wrote to you. And here we find ourselves again, after so much time has passed, worn-out, grown-up, in the same type of relationship. What have you achieved if not successfully replicating the only type of relationship you know and can control? What is this if not being a slave to the holy scriptures of psychoanalysis?

The boundaries you've entrenched yourself in are flashing their warning lights, and I don't think you yourself know who you are, the woman behind the red and purple lines outlining the map of your body.

Who sings you lullabies, Ella? No, not now, but once, long ago. I know you won't answer me. I know I'm intruding again, but you're quite the little intruder yourself. It always drove me crazy to hear mothers sing "Sleep, sleep" as if to get revenge on the absent father, the one who's "gone to work," who "went to the vineyards," who "went to the orchard," the father who will "return when the moon comes out." But everyone knows the father won't be back before the child falls asleep, so for the child it's like he's vanished into thin air. And what the mom's really telling her child is: we don't need him, your father who thinks that going to work is more important than being here with us, but hush, don't fret, I know exactly what you need. Know that no man can recover from such a harsh, fundamental blow, as the mothers' revenge on the absentee father. It was only a few years ago that I realized that to give justice to that song it could be sung only by a father. I happened to be at my friend Itai's house when he was tucking his kids in. Remember Itai? I told you about him. The lawyer who manages somehow to be self-confident and insecure at the same time? And when he sang it, I realized that if you want to make sure that song doesn't cause damage, only a dad can sing it because only then does it become a nurturing song about care and concern, about him coming home early from work, and the present he brings is actually the song itself, the voice, and the melody, and then sweet sound sleep shall come.

Look, you turned me into your child, and that's exactly the opposite of what I wanted to be. I wanted to be your man, your shoulder to lean on, the one you turn to when you're in need, the one who fucks you, the one who fondles your breasts, the one who you know can hurt you but who shows you mercy because he loves you. And what exactly would have happened if just once, you'd gone with me and experienced how you operate in a relationship in which you are a weak and a needy woman? Even now, with one eye and a bum leg, you venture to find some noble women's society and leave the men out. So what do you think that means?

Ella, right from the get-go I felt as though you were reading my mails as long strings of partial objects. The only place you really ever listened to me was in therapy, the soothing echo of your cave, your "sleep, sleep," in which you're the mother singing to the patient. You base your relationship with your patients on the fact that you'll always be there for them, unlike the other figures in their life. And there too, in therapy, I noticed your every breath, and after all, that is almost all you really need.

And Naomi. For the past two weeks she's been asking me to stop calling her Numi, she feels it's infantilizing, that deep down I belittle her. That I belittle everyone. And I don't understand how she caught that deep underlying quality, because nothing I have done could have ever pointed to it. Maybe it's like the magic of therapy, that after some time together our mental and biological mechanisms register the person in front of us and we just know something deep about what is interacting between us.

I can already feel the void of her absence. Even though we are still together, eating, sleeping, talking, the delicate tissues connecting us have detached, and I have no idea how to reattach them. So quickly the suicidal thoughts emerge, so tenuous are the fibers of my life. And I want to shout at her, don't leave, you are not to leave, but I have nothing to base that shout on, because this desire isn't truly mine, and I wish I could be like that friend who sat and begged his wife for an entire year until she agreed to come back.

You are to blame for all of it. My world was perfectly fine until you sent that email, and now, now everything is falling apart again. I'm writing this not with anger but with resignation that this is how it must be. And yet. You are the reason Naomi is leaving. Leaving while still here.

And here is something for you, Uli: Uli, I hope your hands, the ones that caress Ella, that tend to her, will stand in for mine. If there is anything you two need from Israel, please don't hesitate.

Itamar

67

Uli writing on Ella's behalf:

Itamar,

Uli must read me your email over and over, because by the time I think I know how to respond, I fall back into our muddle. I'm not scared of what Uli might see, I **want** her presence to change things between us, to breathe air amongst us. And I mentioned the Swiss police and the board of psychologists more as a lark, I truly was. Because this has nothing to do with human laws, whether of my own invention or of the invention of higher, wiser councils. Not anymore.

It has to do with the boundaries of reality, and what simply cannot be done. Because not everything is possible, Itamari. And that's what both of us, each in our own manner, tried so desperately to rise against. I fought my inherent loneliness in so many ways, you included, but I can't escape the eternal covenant I've made with the people of the kayaks in their little flimsy shells. Whereas you, Itamar, do you know upon which boundaries of life you declared war?

I feel at the tips of my raw nerves how you've just raised a skeptical eyebrow at this. Have you? Still, I'll say that my way of coping has to do with the search for something truthful. Something accurate and real. I want to agree to live my life to the fullest, but also as it is. It doesn't have to be a life devoid of color or boldness, a life without play. But I must finally acknowledge that I can't do everything; I can't go back over relationships and relive them, I can't force my body to function properly, I will never bear another little human being inside me. And I can't be in a romantic relationship with a man who was once my patient. Our different starting points are disruptive to something fundamental, which can't morph or disappear. That's just how it is. I would like to honor the fact that life has spoken, the verdict is in, not everything can be won.

In any event, that's not what I wish for you, Itamari. I wish you a fresh and genuine relationship, one that is spirited, sometimes frustrating, just like the one you have with Naomi. So let go of my breasts and go fondle a viable pair, the right pair. I told Uli to delete this last sentence, but If I know her, she doesn't follow instructions. Fuck it, I hate being dependent on Uli's editing.

On the same topic, it's two eyes and a bum leg, at least for now, thank you very much. You've asked about the things that frighten me, well, they are an odd jumble of the petty and the pivotal; will I wear ridiculous ensembles of clothes? Will I be scared inside my own loneliness? Will I grow old women's facial hair which I won't be able to pluck? Will patients still want to come to therapy? Will they want me to listen to them with ears that will double and triple in their sensitivity? Does one's hearing really become so heightened? What do you think – does the body compensate for deficiencies? What will keep people around me? A sense of duty? True love? The blood relations you're so fond of? What?

As for our bible segment, I'll tell you that in the past few days I've been thinking a lot of the beautiful verse "Even though I walk through the valley of the shadow of death, I will fear no evil." What the hell were they thinking? You bet I will fear evil, until the last flicker of light in the darkness, I will. And yes, I remember how it ends, "for you are with me," and to that I reply: thanks honey, but I'm fine.

68

I don't know where you draw the strength from.

Uli, if you are reading this now to our Ella, please let your hands be mine for a moment, let your fingers be mine and hug her for me, wrap yourself around her for me. Give her a kiss for me. It is true, you do create a space between us, and you are already present. Please write a few words about yourself, because I feel that you know me inside out and I don't know you at all, or Nina, who's there in the background somewhere, maybe listening, maybe taking an interest, will you write to me about her too?

Ella, this whole thing is very confusing. How should I act with you? What can I say to someone who is waging an existential battle? There's some kind of hierarchy here, an imbalance. Your weakness, the body's betrayal, positions you higher up the ladder of our ongoing conversation, since you know something I don't – you can already catch the whiff of death, can taste it. Am I right? It's drawing nearer, and that feeling of being so close to it, is perhaps the most meaningful thing any human being can experience.

Sometimes I don't know how to write to you anymore. Because it would be awful if I said something to hurt and weaken you against this fucking illness. But you're actually doing alright. Despite all the people who came to your aid and all those unbelievable sentences about your sickness and your coping, woven warp and weft into the things you tell Uli to write to me, I feel that it's the same Ella. You're there. I'll just try to be myself. Anyway, if I tried anything else you'd smell the pretense from a mile away.

And that, no disease can take from you, and in that, you're still you, the body's betrayal only heightens that ability.

I just won't accept it. I won't, you hear me? I won't accept the boundaries of reality, won't make peace with them, because the moment I say I can, I'll become a robot. It isn't about the fear of living a small or pathetic life. The thing is that the moment you give up on testing your boundaries, you give up on the desire to know who you truly are. This isn't a hypothetical question, it isn't exploring something that's in a different galaxy, that exists in a completely different environment. It's not far-fetched like waking up one morning and deciding I'm now a hitman or a fighter pilot. You need to reach out for those things that are just an inch beyond your grasp. My hand, for instance, stops within an inch short of working for a humanitarian organization, doing good, sleeping with a man, being in a relationship with two women, separately, together. Maybe for you the possibility of being in a relationship with two men or bringing another child into the world is on a different solar system, distant desires. I see you, Ella the huntress, firing an arrow into the distance. But then, midway, you fetch the arrow and put it back in your quiver. You never go where the arrow takes you. And what about other patients? How come you never slept with a patient? Have you ever thought about it? Wait, maybe you did sleep with one...

You talk about our different starting points, and all that resurfaces is your arrogance. You've been patronizing me since the very beginning, there's no point denying it. I never really stood a chance. The moment someone (meaning me) comes to you for a consultation he automatically is not man enough for you, not strong enough for you, he'll forever remain a weakling in need of a mother. That weakness terrifies you, as you yourself want a mother, someone to take care of you. And that's fine, just living is hard enough, so to be daring, bold, living on the edge? It isn't for you, I know. And who am I to talk? I only challenged the bound-aries of reality a little, too little, and even then, I felt that I was hovering between life and death. I'm a coward. Maybe as much a coward as you. Because once an attempt is imprinted on the body, it's very difficult to go back there. And I won't go back. Not there. Not to that thin line between the land of the living and the land of the dead.

For a moment I forgot it's you I'm talking to, you who's in treatment, who's being forced to examine the one true boundary. To which Ella was I talking to just a moment ago? Never mind.

Uli, if Ella isn't doing well, please don't read her the following lines.

Naomi left two days ago.

Your ability to insinuate yourself in my life and take control of it is truly amazing. Even when you're in Switzerland, even when you can't see and can barely walk. You see how powerful you are? Because you don't need eyes for that, you need a heart that feels.

Yesterday I wanted to kill myself. I called Sarah. Jeff picked up, I had to beg him to bring Sarah to the phone. She was cold and curt, as if the Sarah I knew had become an empty shell. She dismissed me as if I was some pesky fly. And it's a direct result of what happened between us, Jeff must have discovered that Sarah and I slept together. All I remember now is her smell, a light floral perfume with undertones of old age filtering through. She has soft skin, you know? When it comes to Sarah, there's a type of male-female intimacy you can't even imagine. She did tell me: "You can't even see how destructive you are".

Then she wished me well, like some commander discharging a wayward soldier, and I felt, and still feel, scolded and disgusted with myself. I don't understand this life, I don't understand you people, willing to invest in maintaining the illusion of normalcy. Everything is meaningless except those moments when there's a connection, a body touching a body, a consciousness touching a consciousness. And that's what's tearing me apart inside, I'm still waiting for someone who won't come, and if he does – he'll flash before me, blind me and walk away, leaving me devoid of substance, a nobody, a single breath before the great nothingness. So why don't you have a child, Ella, I'll make a baby with you. He'll be ours, and we'll call him Eitan, as in the Hebrew word for strong. And strong he will be. Stronger than us. He'll climb trees, dig up clumps of earth, he'll be connected to the here and now, to the body, to the soul.

I know all your excuses. In therapy, you showed up for me and I showed up for you, and that's what created the bond. But in life I need to show up for myself and you need to show up for yourself. And what will happen between us will be wonderful and real. And still, it sends shivers down my spine to imagine such an encounter, if only I give you a child, if only we call him Eitan. He'll be born and a moment later I'll take off, so you won't kill me.

If I make it till then.

If you make it till then.

Naomi left two days ago, have I told you already?

69

Uli writing on Ella's behalf:

It appears that all of you have decided to lose your marbles at the same time. Uli making her own decisions about what to write on my behalf and what to read me, Nina reading to me what was added or edited out, the same Nina who's been flirting with every doctor and nurse within a one-mile radius and reporting in detail things I didn't even know are possible, and you... you...

I don't understand exactly what happened with your Naomi, and it saddens me a great deal. I wish I could sit down with you and try to make sense of it. And I know you attribute great powers to me, an ability to tear down or elevate with a single breath, and maybe I did send my witchcraft to your faraway land, and maybe I do make you crazy.

If I was on the clock, I'd say that all of you just can't help but behave wildly, so as to make me stop this collective absurdity, and in that, prove to you that I'm still around. Because you can't bear the weakness that has settled inside me, and against my impending blindness you make sure that I'll see.

So much energy is being wasted on fighting the reality of things, on preserving folie à deux, à trois, à quatre... What isn't possible, Itamari? What do you suppose human beings **should** accept? Because I'm starting to feel this is some twisted version of my mother; her entire life devoted to imaginary illnesses, to trains that might spin off their tracks, to a fire that would set the ghetto, we were never in, ablaze. While you Itamari, captivated by Andrew reaching the shores of New Zealand, one last effort before collapsing into his wife and son's arms, when will you agree to live the life that is to be lived?

As to little Eitan, I think the two of us have already given birth to a man who can be quite strong and charming. Let him be. And enough already with that bullshit about sleeping with Sarah, because sometimes things are just painful and lacking, and that's the way they stay. You see, feeling miserable in Feinberg's office doesn't entail finding Freud's lost pages there. Being institutionalized in a psychiatric hospital is tough enough, it doesn't change if you call it a prank, pretending to pop in for a moment to make it more believable. And when Naomi takes her love away, it is missing. You just miss it.

Dear God, who's going to help you take in everything I just said? You're not in therapy, and you're clearly off your meds. Uli is returning to Tel Aviv tomorrow, and we will think of something. I'll ask her to think of something.

From Nina:

The treatment isn't working. We'll be back soon as well. Hang in there.

70

What do you mean the treatment isn't working? Why are you coming back? Why can't you be more specific? I don't get it, why is it so hard to write a few more words about the situation so as not to leave people hanging? Of course I'm off the meds. When I'm on them I'm like an obedient student, attending a class in proper, good civics, cuffed in the chains of my consciousness, listening but not exactly participating. Without them I feel like my real self, sharp, impatient, but me, within the range of my ability to engage with the world, and I don't understand the point of increasing that range through meds if they just dial you down to a frequency that inhibits true engagement. Why talk in slogans, what's going on, what does it mean the treatment isn't working?

Ella, Uli, Nina, remember I told you about my first suicidal thoughts when I was seventeen? I hated trees, water, flowing hair, anything that reminded me of life. You told me that being an existentialist at twenty was the same as being a Communist at twenty, a natural, even essential stage of development. But now, at my age, existentialism poses as real danger. You were right, it's like Sisyphus right before he collapses and falls off the mountain, a last surge of energy before the great fatigue, the void. I mourn you three. And myself too. My neighbor jumped off his parents' balcony a few days ago. They told his kids he fell. Smoked a cigarette and fell. And they think kids buy that bullshit. The guy's lying in the ICU with a spinal injury, and they're disgracing him and his kids with fairytales. All those religious zealots, those who recite with great reverence "isgadal ve'iskadash shmey raba"*, are exalting the one they believe is responsible for their suffering. They're liars. They're breaking the commandment "Thou shalt not bear false witness against thy neighbor." I thought I'd already bid you farewell, had already mourned our relationship, but I still feel that sharp, pulsing pain, making me soft and then hard, sad and angry. What kind of man do you think we birthed together? This Itamar who's writing to you right now? You didn't give birth to me, you are not God, not my god anyway. And you haven't given birth to anything with me except dust and a chase after the wind.

So this is what lovemaking means to you; because what does making a baby mean to you three if not creating new men out of the broken, injured ones who arrive at your doorstep, creating a strong, charming man out of the nothingness sitting in front of you. Yes, you had immense power, and like the light of a dying star I can still feel it guiding me. And still you contradict yourself, on the one hand denying your power and on the other claiming you created me, a display of megalomania and insecurity in the same breath. That's the damage imaginary boundaries cause, they enhance your power while allowing you to deny it.

Do you have any idea how I loved you, Ella? You were mine, nights on end I imagined beating the shit out of any man who touched you, who dared to take what was mine, spraying him with a machine gun, inflicting upon him the worst type of pain. But don't get me wrong, these fantasies have nothing to do with the lies I've told you. My insane love for you was my way of not touching the palpable world, of burrowing into myself. And at the end of the day, how many lies did I tell you? What fraction of them were really fantasies? Jess is Jess and my assault an assault, at least that I can acknowledge. And why are you making light of

---

* "Exalted and hallowed be His great Name" – the opening of the Mourner's "Kadish".

163

my finding the lost manuscript, that I of all people, poor in deeds, freed from the asylum? I crossed the line at least once, I broke the law, assaulted, stole, defied the double standard that allows those in positions of power to accumulate even more power and suppress the weak. I brought light to whoever needed it.

And here I am, talking to you as if you were healthy, as if we were in a relationship. More than anything else that happened in these past two years, it's the image of our meeting in New York that's settled in the middle of my forehead like a fresh bruise. It's a tender pain, a tattoo on the soul, beautiful, hideous, a pain I savor with a sweetness that is second to none. It's true, I didn't sleep with Sarah, I never laid hands on the generator of your nuclear reactor, rerouting the power in my direction. You can attribute one more lie to me. But at least I challenged you. And who are you to lecture me about escapism, even from your lofty seat of sickness? My coarse reality is comprised of shekels, pennies, of desperate appeals to the bank, of buying milk from the loose change between the couch cushions, of the contempt I have for myself and that others have for me, and people like me, who can't take care of themselves, can't make the necessary calculations or gain the upper hand in the simplest of negotiations. And that gulf between us, the one I wanted to bridge through a child, lies precisely between your ability to look the world straight in the eye and tell it "This is mine, I deserve it and I'm taking it," and the fact that everything slips through my fingers. Nothing stays in my possession. You have money precisely because you wouldn't give me any, precisely because you told me "no," nicely, decently, but still "no."

And what about you? Suddenly it dawned on me that everything I just wrote was an attempt to halt the train of thought that has been veering out of control since you wrote me that the treatment failed. What does this mean? That you'll eventually be completely blind? That your life is at risk?

I proposed creating a life together, and you turned me down. Once again, you were right, but not for the reasons you think. Not because we'd already created something together, but because you can't create life out of death, it simply can't be done, and the wise body, the mind, the eggs, the sperm, would know this, and nothing living would come out of us.

I'm drained.

I have nothing more to contribute to this world, and the world, it too erased me from its records. I'm invisible. Naomi didn't leave because of you, Ella, she left because I lost what little self-respect I still had, and you were the last thing I was still hanging onto.

My dear, despised Ella. I'm plotting my death. Slowly, judiciously, calculatingly.

My life has been a gradual loss of control, of resistance. I intend to control my final moments on this planet.

No. This time I'm spot-on. I'm looking in the mirror, I see a tear rolling down my cheek, and I look away. I can feel it sliding down and landing on the edge of my upper lip. I'm mourning myself. Accepting who I was in the past, who I am in the present.

Now I seek death. And I want us to seek it together. To die with you. Not as a pathetic romantic act, but as a conscious, wise, good decision made by two people who are close, even if they are people who can't share a life, can't be together – together they can stop being.

Uli, Nina, update me on when the three of you are returning to Israel, and when I can come visit. And please don't leave anything out.

71

Nina writing on Ella's behalf:

Itamar, Uli returned to Israel today, and she will arrange for you to see a psychiatrist. I know him and he is very good, I think you would like him. Uli will message you the details soon, and please go see him. We've reached the point at which we have no choice but to change.

Nina and I will be back in a week or so (by the way, Nina is a very interesting artist, a selection of her works will be exhibited soon in a gallery in Paris – this is being typed by Nina of her own accord, as she is tired of you people and your tragedies). When Nina wrote you that the treatment wasn't working, she meant that my illness is advancing as predicted, meaning, they failed to slow down its progression. That's OK, Itamar. I'm simply moving in the direction where everyone is going, no exception here. But you, why are you in such a rush, Itamari? There's really no need to cut in line.

When Nina told me she wrote you that the treatment wasn't working, I immediately thought about your treatment, my treatment of you, and how I wish I could feel that I had succeeded with you. After all, you used to be my "flagship case", the case I frequently brought to peer consultations, mulling over what was standing in our way, what theoretical perspective would benefit us. Is it weird for you to hear these things? Does it sound ridiculous now? I fear there have been too many deviations and wrong turns along our way. And you're so dear to me, Itamar, so important. You know what, I'll tell Nina to write that I truly love you. And even though I can see you now in my mind's eye humming under your imaginary mustache: "Sure she loves me, as a patient, but never as a man, that, she won't allow me," I know that deep down you know these words to be true. As I say them, as Nina is now writing them in my name. Come on, take my words, and do something good with them, something reviving. Since I'm not a fan of the idea "even in their death they were not divided" that you're so bent on. Not at all a fan.

Everything that has happened to us, Itamari, together and apart, let me try and tell our story, what do you care? Just listen from the depths of your childhood to the fairytale about Itamar and Ella.

Once upon a time, many years ago, a knight and a dame joined The Order of Valor. No, not a princess and a dragon, certainly a knight and a dame. Although our knight and dame were surrounded by swamps of desolation and despair, they were curious and eager as they embarked on a quest to find a life worth living. And although they were so very attentive, utterly attuned to each other, I think I remained somewhat of a mysterious figure to you, a not-entirely-figured-out dame.

That's how our fairytale begins, but it's not how it ends, because somewhere along the way the knight started feeling that the mysterious dame herself might be the solution to his misery. With a slight shift she could spare him an excruciating fate of dismissal and rejection, he believed. And if she truly loved him, she would leave the Order with him at once, he declared.

It was not a strange desire at all, Itamari, yet the dame knew that their kind of love must never leave fairytale land. So she tried fiercely to envelop the injured knight in her warmth, and pleaded with him to continue their journey, to believe that he himself holds the potion of his life. But she failed. It was a miserable failure, each strenuous word torn into shreds, every sentence shattered, while love dissolved under poisonous heavy rains.

In an act viewed by the knight as a faded remnant of his honor, he sailed away to a distant new land. But they didn't really part. The furious knight continued to cast his dread her way, and she heard. She heard him on those cold lonely nights and came to him, but it wasn't enough to heal the bruises in his soul.

The years passed; dark vines wound around her heart in old fairytale land. And when the dame grew very weak, she called the knight onto her deathbed. A quick and bitter night, it was, as our words met at bay. There, my whole-broken figure was revealed to you, all my shards lying silently between us. Will you take at least this from me? My intact belief that we can be immensely injured and still somehow stand, alive, and hoping?

The buzz of a bee woke me up in the middle of the night. In this intermediate twilight I hallucinated that there's a beehive inside the ancient wall, and soon the wall will collapse on me, and the bees will break free. I'm not exactly scared; I feel that it's right. Dreams are hiding inside the wall, as are hallucinations, and the protective wall is thin.

72

It's hard to figure out these pants, how to put them on. Two long sleeves for the legs, funny. I decided to go commando today, because I need to go to the post office and it seemed too unrelated, letters and underwear. I wonder who's sent me a package. Must be one of the magazines I've subscribed to in the past two months. If I don't have a community, I'll make one myself. Now, for instance, I'm part of the community of people who go commando. My phone and I, we're a very close-knit community. We make lists, prepare, prepare, prepare, the sky is gray today and it's making me tremble with pleasure. The moment you decide to stop living, the simplest of actions takes on such a force. Chopping a tomato is such a juicy thing, the crystals of instant coffee are so beautiful, so fascinating, the fridge is making noises, actually talking, maybe even singing, and speaking to yourself becomes an inseparable part of you, because every thought about the moment you'll cease to exist makes it clearer that you'll be surrounded. Not by some fence you can imagine skipping over or cutting a hole through and... bam! you're on the other side, suspended in some thick liquid, nothing to your right and nothing to your left, and that'll be your world from then on and to eternity, no world at all.

And then you linger there, you become so claustrophobic it knocks you down. And you're already down, on the ground. What a word, c-l-a-u-s-t-r-o-p-h-o-b-i-a. I'm working it in my mouth, tasting it. There's so much to do. So little time. My to-do list almost makes me happy: buy a syringe, get the material, my health potion, the one that will be inside me, press record, tidy up Orly and Danny's beautiful apartment on 23 Borochov Street, get the living room ready for the event, the event with a capital E, the armchair, Uli would cross her legs slowly, how it drove me crazy when she did that, then she'd pull both legs onto the armchair and talk to me like the girlfriend I've never had, I'd bang my head against the wall after those meetings, complaining about this fucking life, oh, and to have someone in this world who'd answer me, not for a moment, not a fleeting flash, but for a day, a week, a month, no, it's Ella who drove me crazy with her legs and her cleavage, yes, Ella, Nina is the artist, the one I'm supposed to meet as a void, as a nothing. Dogs are such beautiful, noble creatures, they look you straight in the eye, without cheating, their paws are a work of art, people are the ridiculous ones, they dress up, groom themselves, it's all human experimentation, I laugh in the middle of the street, people look, let them look, today Milgram's experiment wouldn't have passed the Helsinki Committee, I remember that lesson so well, the people in lab coats saying quietly, "It is absolutely essential that you continue," and the participants cranking the voltage all the way up despite the shrieks of the person on the other side of the glass wall. Is there anything more human than that experiment? No, there isn't, that's the brink, Milgram is smearing humanity all over our bodies, exposing our own lack of boundaries, the wickedness of it all. I see people on the street and I mumble, you, you and you are dangerous, I'm telling you the truth, how nicely the women are dressed, neatly combed, make-up on, you're dying to carry out orders and you have no boundaries, do you get how dangerous you are? And that experiment wouldn't have been approved today, but psychological therapy, that's fine. The billboards are so beautiful, the herbal tea so colorful and fruity, really mesmerizing, the tomato soup hot, steamy, bubbling, and people go into this experiment with their eyes open, I know I did. You asked me during our first meeting why I came to you, and

I answered: "I'm depressed, everything's stuck, at a standstill, so I came to play with my life with eyes wide open, because what I've had so far isn't really a life," and that's something they can't take away from you, whoever you are, Sarah, Jess, Ella, Nina, you're all cunts, every last one of you.

What did I want to get in this shop? I know I walked in because I needed something here, they have toothbrushes, floss, combs, no, I don't believe you're the leader of the experiment, that what you did was a manipulation to test my boundaries, or that you pretended to be the electrocuted subject, as if you were in pain, otherwise it never would have worked. You see, Nina, you beautiful, talented, charming high-heeled woman, part of what disappears when the nectar of the gods enters your body is that miraculous thing, the mechanism that can't be restored, that recognizes when someone else is being tortured, that you're his torturer, controlling his pain, what are you talking about, what the hell are you talking about? Someone's approached me asking if everything is alright, and I told him yes, yes, everything's fine, I'm just looking. I cry in movies, and you yourself said we were in a movie, in a book, why not, a knight and a dame, and if only I accepted your story, accepted the notion that all my suffering stems from the primal rejection, then maybe you could, but something went wrong in your game, I became attached to you, and while you were talking to me, from within your body and soul, I filled the space between us with more and more honey and beeswax, waiting for the day you'd try to get up from your chair and say, Oh, that's odd, it won't move, and you'd look around and see me inside a room filled with orange beeswax, a worker bee, and you're the queen bee that will never fly, because that's exactly what happened, you played and I agreed to take part in the experiment, it was the unwritten condition we agreed on, and we've been apart for some time now, that I know as I stand here, in what seems to be a pharmacy but there are so many strange things about it, have you ever been here? I'm just trying to stay human, to tell myself that every relationship I've ever had was meaningful, and that if I undo it or walk away from it I'll be doomed, and the relationship with Nina, no, Ella, no, Uli, funny how similar the names are, is the most important relationship you've ever had, so don't ignore it, people move their mouths and a voice comes out and they talk, everybody around me is talking, and it seems they understand each other, it's the body, for sure, the eyes, the corners of the mouth, a smile is something that goes beyond the natural, from where I'm at it seems like something divine, the miraculous connection between the consciousness and the mind, and what made my life here on earth tolerable and sometimes even beautiful.

What was I going to buy? See, even from where you're at, a steadily worsening disability, you keep up the appearance of beauty, you've already forgotten what you told me, to tell it like it is, you didn't keep your promise, don't cry, I only hope there's someone to whom you do tell it like it is, or at least to yourself, because even now I don't really know how you're doing, and if this is your way of protecting me, then know it's doomed to failure. I'm a small figure at the entrance to a pharmacy, from a bird's-eye view I'm a strip of color next to other strips of color, a strip talking to himself. And more strips are added and subtracted over time, dots, lines, can you see? Look, you'll see it. I'm writing while walking around and the doorbell of this strange pharmacy is ringing incessantly, I'm writing and eventually I'll press send, and I hope I'll feel comfortable in Danny and Orly's living room, they're abroad right now and will be back only a few days after the event.

I feel the fringes of my body, my skin enveloping me, hear the blood pulsing through my veins, I understand my separateness as simple, fundamental and deep matter. I know you wrote about our separateness but I'm asking you now, in the name of that separateness, not to blame yourself, I've made this decision all by myself. Have you ever noticed how many sounds are carried through the air, dishes clanking, wheels grinding, engines rattling, the quiet behind them all is unbearable, and now I can hear it sometimes. Something has calmed down inside me now, as I'm writing you. Something has come to a halt. Our relationship has slightly postponed the inevitable, illuminated that which could not be spoken, and let it speak. And it was important, sometimes it was my entire being. Oh, Ella, suddenly I realize how strong I am, I could have moved mountains, could have brought them down, may the Lord bless you and guard you, may the Lord make His face shed light upon you and be gracious unto you, may the Lord lift up His face unto you and give you peace.

73

Wait for me there, 23 Borochov Street, Givatayim. I hope at least that much is true. You will wait for me there, alive.

74

Ella handwriting outside the ICU at Ichilov hospital:

20:05

I'll write you this nightly protocol, and when you recover, I'll make you read it. Every single word of it. Tell me, was it necessary to swallow all that garbage, and then invite me over just to find you on your friends' carpet? Did you want me to drag you here, with the help of a petrified taxi driver? Was this absolutely essential?

20:28

This thing you've done, trying to off yourself, what does it mean? I've read your explanations and I don't know what to think: are you telling me through your body how separate we are? Or that we've never been as bound to each other as we are right now – thin threads of flesh connecting our souls continue to bleed?

21:46

Maybe you think I'm the old blind Tiresias who knows the secret of Oedipus's misfortune and in a moment of anger divulges it. Maybe you think I'm Oedipus, who in his blindness gained enlightenment. But I just can't see very well.

22:12

I have no more secrets from you. I used to have a private life, but I unjustly handed it over to you, along with Sarah and Jeff, Uli and Nina. You refused the appointment that Uli arranged for you,

175

remember? And Nina already took off to her exhibition in Paris. I'm the only one left. The crossed legs are mine.

23:05
Pnina the head nurse just asked me who your emergency contact is. I gave her your parents' names, I don't know what you'd make of it, but I had too. I also said I'm your psychologist, can you believe it, Itamar? Now, I'm your psychologist.

23:52
Itamar, Itamar, Itamar, what will I do about us? You're hovering between life and death, as if you can be in two places at once, as if the two are one and the same. But there are differences. Between us, between roles and generations, between what's allowed and what's forbidden, between what can and cannot be.

00:26
The letters I scribble are jumbled. Have you ever seen the hand-writing of a person who's almost blind? And finding the bathroom here is such an ordeal, so I'm stuck in my spot. Maybe I'll ask the nice young nurse to help me in a bit. She really is cute, you'd agree if you were awake, but I might have ruined your chances with her, as I didn't correct her when she addressed me as your wife. Psychologist wife, just as you dreamed it would be.

01:55
You know, before that damn trip to Switzerland I tried to get a few things done around the house. I sorted boxes of "memories" for hours on end, and I was doing a very poor job. My sweet girls tried to help me, but at some point they too realized it was hopeless. What-ever I tried to box up burst open, revealing more and more gaping holes from my past. Long story short, I didn't throw anything out,

just stored the papers and objects in new graves, beautiful floral boxes from Ikea. Now I'm thinking, maybe it's okay that I couldn't throw anything out. Maybe every house needs a crawl space, a walk-in closet, a basement, if not an attic. Maybe every mind needs a subconscious, maybe things are supposed to stay this way, somewhat unresolved. And what do I care what I leave behind, what they find in these boxes after I'm gone.

02:40
I want to make sure your liver is working, that it can withstand all the garbage you swallowed, and then I'll drag myself home to sleep. I'll sleep and sleep until you recover, or until I forget it all.

03:27
Itamari, it's not God I'm mocking when I say "thanks honey, but I'm fine." It's us humans I pity, who like children ask with feeble voices and soft gazes, for someone to show up.

04:02
Itamari, they told me you're stable, although it's still unclear how much damage you caused your liver. They let me sneak a peek at you, hooked up to IVs and machines, so small...

04:47
On my way home I thought of a poem I love, about the faraway land of Oz. I looked it up for us, tell me what you think of its beautiful ending:
"No matter if in Oz it happens, or in a high and loftier place. No matter matters anymore, except that once, just once upon a time Ours was a time of grace, when we were peaceful and forgotten, like a pair of clocks that halted mid pace."*

---

* "In the Faraway Land of Oz" by Aryeh Sivan; translated by Miriam Yahil-Wax.

75

Ella,

I'm writing you in tears, writing and crying. My child is gone.

My child is gone, and now I'm writing from his email, and you'll receive a message with his name next to it as if he were still among the living. I'm trying to find a reason, a lead, for God's sake, I didn't get to say goodbye. His father went to identify the body, they spared me the sight. It's so hard to imagine him lifeless, since he was always gushing with life, a wellspring, even when he wasn't mentally sound. How could he have done such a thing to himself. To us. Such a tragedy.

I read your correspondence from the end to the beginning, reading the end so close to it, so alive, it was intensely difficult for me. I feel a horrible rage, you could have informed us, Itamar showed you all the signs and you just kept dragging him down.

They told me at the hospital that you appointed yourself as his contact when you were here yesterday. Who do you think you are? Don't come to the funeral, Ella, and don't come to the Shiva. You are not welcome.

Next to the computer there's a letter for you as well as the will, which I'm only attaching because you were mentioned in it. It is with a heavy heart that I'm sending it. You don't deserve to be mentioned in it. You do not deserve it.

Nurit

76

Where are you now, Ella? What are you feeling? Can you sense that these are my last moments on earth? Was our bond strong enough for you to feel my disappearance? I want to believe it was. That there's something in this world greater than the sum of its parts. I hope it will show you kindness, this world, more kindness than it has shown so far.

Now I can see things crystal clear. I rearranged the furniture a bit, to feel that I left my mark on the room. I'm noticing the details. The bookcase is a bit crooked, I can feel the weight of the shelves, there's a burnt lightbulb in the lamp above me.

It's so surprising that love is founded on fiction, on one's ability to observe reality, to acknowledge it and then distort it as one pleases... this is also true of the love born in therapy.

Some would say: "In the beginning there was touch, then came the relationship." I say: "The touch was primeval, the touch is the relationship." I caress myself. This is me. This is my foot. Here's the chafed skin on my ankle, here's the little finger that strays from the others. All my obsessions will die with me, all of them are nothing compared to nature's beauty and cruelty. No matter. No harm done. The murmur of the sea the saltiness of the wave the dread

Last Will and Testament

Since no man knows his last day, but his end is known, and if the word is near him, in his mouth and in his heart, to observe it.

And whereas it is my wish to write a will and express my last wishes and directions as to what will be done with me and my estate after my passing.

Therefore I, Itamar Enoch, residing at 5 Maale Haakrabim St., Tel Aviv, being of sound mind and memory, out of my own good, free will, and not being actuated by any duress, menace, fraud, mistake, or undue influence, hereby declare:

1. This is my last will which is a witnessed will according to the directions of the Inheritance Law 1965, and it is fully valid and binding according to the laws of the State of Israel, my residence and domicile, and it applies to all my estate of any kind and anywhere.
2. I hereby expressly revoke all other wills made by me, in writing or by heart, and there is no validation to any other will made by me until this day.
3. I hereby request that DR. Ella Ziv handle all arrangements concerning my funeral and body. These shall be carried out according to her discretion, or the discretion of a representative she appoints.
4. I hereby leave the rights to my manuscript, "It Speaks for Itself" to Dr. Ella Ziv, and all matters regarding publication to her discretion.

5. I hereby direct to restore Sigmund Freud's manuscript, currently in Dr. Ella Ziv's possession, to its rightful owner, Dr. Feinberg from New York. It is my final request that an effort be made, whether by Dr. Ella Ziv or Dr. Feinberg, to publish my discovery of said manuscript, as well as an effort to make said manuscript accessible to researchers and professionals. For the record, the circumstances in which I came to obtain said manuscript have absolutely nothing to do with Dr. Ella Ziv.

6. To Ms. Naomi Tzur, who was with me in innocence and grace, I leave my books and moveable property.

7. I hereby direct that my provident fund at Ayalon Insurance serve to pay out any debts in my account at Bank Hapoalim, branch 683. I bequeath the remainder of my residuary estate to my parents, Nurit and Avigdor Enoch.

8. I appoint my parents, Nurit and Avigdor Enoch, as administrators of my estate and will.

In witness whereof I have affixed my signature,

Itamar Enoch

Tel Aviv, 6 November 2015, 24 Cheshvan, 5776

We, the undersigned witnesses,

1. Yosef Ben Margalit and Reuven Lulus
2. David Ben Rachel and Baruch Fuerlicht

Hereby confirm that this instrument was signed and acknowledged by the testator, Mr. Itamar Enoch, ID no. 02673845, as his

Last Will and Testament in our presence, and we, at his request, and in his presence, and in the presence of each other, have subscribed our names as witnesses.

All of which is attested to this, 6 November 2015, 24 Cheshvan, 5776

77

You fool. You foolish fool. Why did you do it? Undo it. Let me come save you, you know that I can.

Because what on earth will I do without us?

Uli once said to me: "Notice how time after time he takes all his wisdom and daring and charm and starts going nuts." "He's protecting the two of you," she continued, "so you won't get even more entangled than you already are."

Is that true Itamari? Because you don't have to do it anymore. I promise.

Come back, stand at my doorway and say, "Hello, I'm Itamar, I'm here for therapy." Walk into my room and repeat all the things you've said to me. I'll be a very mature psychologist, quiet and calm, and I'll find the right way to be near you.

Will you do only this Itamar?

A few years ago, before I knew the disease would return, I visited the "Dialogue in the Dark" exhibition. Have you been? Don't answer, it's my turn now. At the entrance to the exhibit there's a thin light that fades into darkness. I remember the dread that came over me, the feeling of doom, the loneliness. The people in my group managed quite well, found their way in the dark, but I couldn't. I stood rooted to my spot, and to my complete surprise, started crying. Quiet whimpers that turned into loud sobs. Our guide heard me. He called me over to him.

"I can't," I told him, wailing, "I don't know where you are."

"You can," he said quietly. "Listen. You can hear where I am."

"Come here," I told him. "I can't."

"Listen to my voice, I'll keep talking to you. Just listen and follow."

One hesitant, self-effacing step, then back to my spot against the wall.

"Can you hear me? I'm here, I'm waiting for you."

I wiped my tears. I started walking. His warm hand met me in the dark.

Acknowledgements

To Amir Gutfreund – who read the first draft, and instantly knew it was possible. You are terribly missed.

To Yair Eldan – my fearless companion to the Land of Oz.

To Edna Freidenberg – who meticulously read the translation with "the charity principle".

To Yaara Shehori and Daniella Zamir – for their bright and lucid voices.

To Michelle Mazor – for precious finds in translation.

To Merav Roth – my generous, clever mother, for following each breadcrumb on my way to bountiful meals.

To Yotam Ziv – who taught me love.

Orna Reuven

www.ingramcontent.com/pod-product-compliance
Lightning Source LLC
Chambersburg PA
CBHW062138020426
42335CB00013B/1248